Preaching Master Class

art for faith's sake series

SERIES EDITORS:

Clayton J. Schmit
J. Frederick Davison

This series of publications is designed to promote the creation of resources for the church at worship. It promotes the creation of two types of material, what we are calling primary and secondary liturgical art.

Like primary liturgical theology, classically understood as the actual prayer and practice of people at worship, primary liturgical art is that which is produced to give voice to God's people in public prayer or private devotion and art that is created as the expression of prayerful people. Secondary art, like secondary theology, is written reflection on material that is created for the sake of the prayer, praise, and meditation of God's people.

The series presents both worship art and theological and pedagogical reflection on the arts of worship. The series title, *Art for Faith's Sake*,* indicates that, while some art may be created for its own sake, a higher purpose exists for arts that are created for use in prayer and praise.

OTHER VOLUMES IN THIS SERIES:

Dust and Ashes by James L. Crenshaw
Dust and Prayers by Charles L. Bartow
Senses of the Soul by William A. Dyrness

FORTHCOMING VOLUMES IN THIS SERIES:

Praying the Hours in Ordinary Life by Clayton J. Schmit & Lauralee Farrer
Teaching Hymnal by Clayton J. Schmit

* *Art for Faith's Sake* is a phrase coined by art collector and church musician, Jerry Evenrud, to whom we are indebted.

Preaching Master Class

Lessons from Will Willimon's Five-Minute
Preaching Workshop

BY
William H. Willimon

EDITED BY
Noel A. Snyder

CASCADE *Books* · Eugene, Oregon

PREACHING MASTER CLASS
Lessons from Will Willimon's Five-Minute Preaching Workshop
Art for Faith's Sake 4

Cascade Books
An Imprint of Wipf and Stock Publishers
199 W. 8th Ave., Suite 3
Eugene, OR 97401

www.wipfandstock.com

ISBN 13: 978-1-60608-915-6

Cataloguing-in-Publication data:

Willimon, William H.

Preaching master class : lessons from Will Willimon's five-minute preaching workshop / edited by Noel A. Snyder

viii + 126 p. ; 23 cm. Includes bibliographical references.

Art for Faith's Sake 4

ISBN 13: 978-1-60608-915-6

1. Preaching. I. Snyder, Noel A. II. Title. III. Series.

BV4211.2 W534 2010

Manufactured in the U.S.A.

Contents

Preface

Like many homileticians, Bishop Willimon believes that preaching is an art, a craft. If such a designation is accurate, however, might we not conclude that the proper way to study preaching is to train with a competent teacher? Students of any art must learn something of the theory, technique, and history of that art in order to find their own place within the artistic community. For most artists, the bulk of such learning happens in their teachers' studios. But to what extent do similar learning opportunities exist for most students of preaching? If preaching is an art, then we have a long way to go in the training of our preachers.

Given the short supply of preaching studios in comparison to other art forms, perhaps the next best thing is for preachers to simulate such training on their own. For years, readers of the quarterly publication *Pulpit Resource* have had the opportunity to simulate studying under Will Willimon through his column, "The Five-Minute Preaching Workshop." The present volume comprises the best selections from that column over the past decade and a half. Taken as a whole, readers of this book have the opportunity to simulate for themselves a master class with this master preacher.

Since these selections were originally published as part of a quarterly homiletical aid for preachers who follow the Revised Common Lectionary, some traces remain of the particular texts and seasons for which the columns were written. Yet I trust that the lessons that originated in those particular circumstances will prove useful for preachers in a variety of present circumstances. In order to highlight Willimon's main homiletical emphases, the selections have been divided into four sections. The first section comprises Willimon's more fundamental reflections on the practice of preaching. In the second section, Willimon addresses some of the special issues that arise in preaching. The third section is made up of those columns that examine preaching in relation to the text, while the selections in the fourth section reflect upon preaching as it relates to the church and the world.

Careful readers will find some of the material repetitive, although such repetition is not likely to surprise those who are familiar with Willimon. When I asked the bishop in conversation about his habit of saying things over again, he appealed to a Karl Barth quotation about the purpose of theology being to repeat oneself. For our present purposes, he could have just as easily appealed to pedagogy. How often do students instantly catch on to what their teachers are trying to teach them?

On that note, welcome to the studio of a master preacher. May you leave equipped to preach God's Word with greater faithfulness and fervency.

Noel A. Snyder

SECTION 1

The Practice of Preaching

Wonder at Words

A number of years ago, I did a book on clergy who call it quits. Burnout. In interviewing pastors who had given up on ministry, I discovered that many of them cited preaching as the most debilitating of pastoral activities. Should I have been surprised?

It can be a tough way to earn a living, giving oneself, week-in-week-out, to the task of bringing God's truth to speech. Preaching is a fragile art. Between eleven and noon on Sundays I cast my words out toward the congregation, they bounce between limestone walls, ricochet off the ceiling, are quickly absorbed, die, and then, silence, all-threatening silence.

Like Israel's loquacious God, I hate silence. I chisel my message out of the hard granite of the biblical text, a text that often refuses to speak without being wrestled to the ground, twisted, wrenched into sound. In the back of my mind I have this haunting fear that one Sunday the text may refuse to speak and I'll be stuck with numbed, dumb silence. It hasn't happened yet, but still, it's enough to keep me nervous.

I mount the pulpit, I throw some words at them. My Sunday listeners sit impassively before me, staring back at me, not as eager to hear as they ought to be. I cast out my voice into the silence; the sermon begins. My voice has the resonance of an old gate swinging by its hinges in the wind. Why do they keep returning every Sunday? What, in God's name, do they hear? It's only words.

I digress.

Augustine referred to himself as a *word merchant*. After three decades of peddling my wares, I know less about the job than when I began. Why do they listen and not hear? Why do I speak but it's only a lecture and not yet a sermon? Why am I so disquieted when they do hear? Who killed last Sunday's sermon—me, them, or the Holy Spirit? But I digress again.

You and I, as preachers, are dealers in words. Words are all that we have to do any important work. Like some of the psalms of lament, I want both to thank God for speech and to blame God for speech being so difficult. And I want to fall in love with language, over and over again. That's one reason why I read poetry, and go to plays and movies, and read all I can, because, as a preacher, it's all just words. I want to love words and, in what I write and edit, to have fellow preachers and listeners love them with me. A preacher is, among other things, someone who has learned to love words.

A student bores me to death with an extended, detailed account of the young woman with whom he is now in love. He loves her for her wit, her sarcasm, her body, her faith, the way she loves him, but above all she is loved for her sheer, mysterious otherness. I love the Word and words in a similar way. I'm exuberant about speech.

Even as I write these words on a page, I'm already nervous that you will not like these words, that they will not do to you what I intend, that you won't understand, worse, that you will understand what I am saying better than I. I will not have concealed that meaning of myself that I thought it unsafe to reveal. Worse, my words will have gotten away from me, broken free in the life of someone I don't even know, made mischief in someone I know only as *my reader*, or taken on a significance I did not intend. When a preacher's words become the Word, it's scary. Such are the perils of the profession of merchant of words, Servant of the Word.

I never quite got over my puerile fascination with the sheer wonder of words, thank God. As a child, my mother bored herself to death with laborious re-readings of *Winnie the Pooh*, and *The Tales of Grimm*, and *Hurlburt's Bible Stories*. When she complained about my infantile obsession with stories, a teacher friend of hers advised, "No child likes that much *Winnie the Pooh* who is not a born lover of words."

I therefore, despite the rigors of this job, have always considered my vocation into the preaching ministry to be a peculiar act of grace. Not only do I get to love language, but I get to do it for a living. Some Christians had to serve God by being eaten by lions. Others had to be celibate. All I have to do is talk.

I'm writing these thoughts on Pentecost, the day that the speech of the church began. You will recall the story as Luke tells it in Acts 2. Having been told by the risen Christ, "You will be my witnesses in Jerusalem, in all Judea, and Samaria, and to the ends of the earth" (Acts 1:8), we don't have to wait long for the Word-generated witnessing to begin. A crowd forms out in the street upset about the inebriation upstairs. "They're doing what they did when Jesus was with them," they scoffed. "They're drunk!"

Peter comes out and speaks. Peter. Do you recall where we left Peter only a short while before? He was in the courtyard with the maid. While Jesus was being whipped and stripped before Pilate, Peter, *The Rock*, the one who had so loudly declared his allegiance to Jesus in the upper room, was stupefied and tongue-tied when confronted by the maid in the courtyard.

The power of that woman! In just a few short verses, she had Peter cursing Jesus, "I don't know the man!"

Now, before a large, mocking mob, Peter comes out and speaks, makes one of the shortest and most effective homilies in all of Scripture, assuring the crowd that "this promise is for you and for your children . . . for everyone whom the Lord Jesus calls."

The Holy Spirit induces, produces speech, specifically, gospel, news that is good. Furthermore, the Holy Spirit produces speakers, those who are genuinely surprised by their guts in standing up and saying a good word for God. By the grace of God, we not only have something to say, but the means to say it, which Christians have always regarded as miraculous gift.

The Most Dangerous, Most Wonderful Step in Sermon Preparation

Over the years, I have come to believe that the most important time, in the movement from the biblical text to the preached sermon, occurs very early in the process of preparation. I have come to believe that the first encounters with the biblical text are the most crucial. This is counter to what I was taught, that our first impressions of a biblical text are usually wrong. Of course, the people saying this were biblical scholars who spent their lives pondering biblical texts, dissecting them, laboriously and minutely examining the text. Therefore, they were convinced that there was no way to be grasped by a biblical text other than the way that they had mastered it. Note that many of them spoke of "mastering" the biblical text. The text was treated as a passive object that we examine and dissect in order to get down to the kernel of the real truth of the text.

Fortunately, we are learning a much more dynamic view of the biblical text. Biblical texts are not only speaking certain ideas, but rather they are engaging us in various experiences. To meet a biblical text is somewhat analogous to meeting another person. While it is true that first impressions are often deceptive, first impressions are also very important. When first meeting another person, the person comes across to us "cold." We have no preconceptions, or past experience with the person, so there is a kind of immediacy in our encounter with that person. Sometimes our first impressions can be very truthful.

I recall a friend who reported to me that upon meeting someone, he felt this person to be smug, arrogant, and full of pride. He got to know this person and the complexity of his personality. He became appreciative of the great erudition of this man. However, he could still say later, "My first impression of him was quite accurate. He is a person full of pride and smugness, despite his other virtues."

A biblical text is a work of art, a piece of literature. Any piece of literature has an immediate impact. Sometimes that immediate impact can be lessened, or defused through detailed work on the piece. Therefore, we ought to retain as much of our first impression as possible.

Furthermore, let us be reminded that our congregations, the people who will actually hear our sermons, have nothing but first impressions to go on in their understanding of the text. I think I have ruined a lot of sermons by trying to unload all of my biblical study of the text on the congregation. The poor congregation had no prior preparation for this. I have spent hours studying this text. The congregation has had the benefit (or the curse) of none of this. Therefore, as a preacher, I ought to strive to maintain my first impression of the text, the freshness with which I encountered it, which will be close to how our congregation will be appropriating the text.

I remember a friend of mine emerging from a class after he had given a lecture, saying, "I failed in that lecture. I knew too much about the subject and completely ruined everything." I think I know what he was talking about. It is possible, through hours of study, to know so much about a text that we cannot talk about that text in the twenty minutes of our sermon. Therefore, first impressions are important.

I advise beginning sermon preparation as early as possible. With the need to preach a sermon on Sunday looming before you like a hangman's noose, we panic. We jump to conclusions too soon. Our preparation begins, not with imaginative exploration, but with a grim prodding toward the end of the sermon.

Eugene Lowry advises,

> Wallow in the text. Read it aloud. Hear it and see it. The mind works differently through the ear and through the eye . . . Do your best to forget that Sunday is coming. Read the text out loud over and over—and in numerous translations and paraphrases. Then say it in your own words. Dive in the deep end of the biblical pools. Get inundated with the biblical word.[1]

It is very important to try to keep as loose as possible during this stage of the process. I find it helpful to keep a sheet of paper in front of me and simply jot down first impressions. I will not want these first impressions to be lost in a mass of later study. Listen for what is strange in the

---

1. Lowry, *The Sermon*, 91–92.

text, out of place, or odd. This weirdness can be helpful as the sermon is later taking form. What is weird to you at first hearing may cease to be weird after you have read and reread the text. So jot down first impressions. Try to stay confused about the text. Don't jump to conclusions too quickly.

Thus, Eugene Lowry has long urged us preachers, when we look at a biblical text, "look for trouble." Try to be open to those matters in the text that you have not noticed before. Intentionally develop the attitude of the little child who drives adults crazy by asking of phenomena, "Why? Why? Why?"

Cultivate a willingness to be shocked, surprised by the text. Of course, it is very difficult to plan to be spontaneous. However, I believe that we can discipline ourselves when we go to a biblical text, to expect to be disarmed and dislodged by the text. You have heard me quote James Sanders, the great biblical interpreter, who said words to the effect, "If you read a biblical text and say to yourself, 'that is what I've always thought,' read the text again. You probably have got the text wrong."

Because God is God and we are not, because God's ways are not our ways, it is reasonable to expect to be surprised by a text.

Eugene Lowry advises us to read a biblical text and underline all of the important portions of the text. Then, after the underlining is complete, go back and look at what is not underlined. Are there sections that I have simply taken for granted? Are there details that I have overlooked in my desire to get the "big" point of the text?

Try taking different positions within the text. When reading the story of the Lord's call to young Samuel when he was living with the priest Eli, try to read the story again from Eli's perspective. How does this text read differently if you are reading it from the perspective of an old priest at the temple as opposed to a young boy? Biblical writers often give us a glimpse of biblical events through the eyes and the words of spectators.

Sometimes, when reading about Jesus, there is that tendency for us to identify with Jesus, to take our place standing beside Jesus. Rather, we ought to take our places within the crowd listening to Jesus, watching his strange behavior, and trying to figure out what is going on. Do free association with a biblical text. Keep stoking the mind with images that are evoked by this particular text.

Eugene Lowry asks, "Why is it that we wake up in the middle of the night with our best insights?"[2] Lowry surmises that perhaps it is because our mind needs room for good insights to bubble to the top. When we drop our consciousness, our means-toward-an-end mentality, our preconscious mind is set loose.

All of this suggests that the most creative stage in sermon preparation, the stage that we must desperately try to keep fresh in our minds throughout our preparation, is the earliest stage, in our first encounters with the biblical text. Fresh, engaging sermons are probably won or lost here in the earliest stages of our preparation.

2. Lowry, *The Sermon*, 99.

Character and Credibility

When Aristotle was offering in his *Rhetoric* the classical treatise of persuading people through speaking, as he listed all of the "available means of persuasion," including reason, emotion, and the character of the speaker, Aristotle listed the character of the speaker as the most important. In fact, a later rhetorician would define a good speech as "a good person speaking well."

Both the opinions of classical rhetoric and contemporary studies of public speaking agree that the personality, the character of the speaker is the key factor in credibility of the speech. You must answer this question if you are to be an effective Christian communicator: How does my personality, my relationship to the listeners, and my character influence the persuasiveness of my preaching? Credibility is a gift that is given to an audience. In all of our speaking, we are seeking to be credible, believable to our hearers. Nevertheless, even though credibility is a gift offered by the audience to the speaker, that does not mean that the speaker has no control over credibility.

At least five factors influence the credibility of a speaker:

1. **Character.** The speaker must be perceived as trustworthy and true. There must be congruence between the listeners' assessment of the personality of the speaker and what the speaker is saying. As a parish pastor, you have great opportunity to influence through character. Your listeners get to know you intimately in the daily activity of the congregation. Of course this can be a two-edged sword! Because they know you so well, in their daily interaction with you as their pastor, then they are apt to pick up phoniness, artificiality, and incongruity between what you say and who they perceive you to be.

2. **Competence.** Your audience must perceive you as a person who has control over the subject.

3. **Composure.** Speakers who are nervous are less trustworthy than speakers who appear confident and composed.

4. **Likeability.** We listen attentively and positively to people for whom we have positive feelings. This can be a great challenge for the Christian communicator. After all, to be faithful to the gospel, at times we must say things that are not likeable, ideas and beliefs that will challenge our hearers, that our hearers hear as criticism. Nevertheless, if our hearers are positively disposed toward us as people, they will receive even our criticism much better than they would if they were negatively inclined toward us.

5. **Extroversion.** Speakers who reach out to their audience are positively perceived by their audience. The audience perceives that the speaker really cares about them, really wants to be heard by them. However, extroverts in public speaking also note that it is possible to be too extroverted. A speaker who seems too intent on pleasing an audience, in being liked by the audience, can be perceived by the audience as disingenuous and artificial. The audience, feeling that the speaker is putting the make upon them, may resist the speaker. Defenses rise when we feel we are about to be manipulated by another person for that person's own ends.

Although most preachers do not stand up and enumerate for the congregation all of their academic degrees, and all of the schools where they have studied, we do have ways of winning the congregation's sense of confidence. We will say things like, "In my study this week of today's scripture, I had a tough task before me." Or we will say, "In my 20 years as a pastor I have found that . . . "

Conversely, credibility can be engendered by the speaker admitting to his or her shortcomings or mistakes. This conveys a sense of candor to the listeners. The speaker says, "One of my weaknesses is that I tend to judge people by their appearance. I will see someone shabbily dressed, and I think that this person is rather shabby. Have you ever done that?" This is particularly true for preachers who are sometimes perceived by their congregations as plaster saints, as people who have solved all spiritual problems for themselves and are now, from their exalted perch of perfectionism, seeking to instruct the congregation. Letting some of our vanity come through in our speech is a means of establishing greater credibility.

Perhaps you are uncomfortable with this talk of strategies for improving your credibility with your audience. Character is something that is a gift, something that we either have, or do not have. True. However, as we said in the beginning, related to our public speaking, a positive perception of our character, credibility, is also a gift bestowed by the audience. Therefore, it is fair for us to use the available means at our disposal for winning the credibility of our audience, for conveying to them our genuine concern to be heard and received by them.

Easter Preaching

Paul says, "If Christ is not resurrected from the dead, then your preaching is in vain." I can certainly see why Paul would say that if Christ is not raised from the dead, then our *faith* is in vain, but why does Paul link the resurrection to our proclamation, Easter to our preaching? Perhaps Paul does this because he knows that there is an integral relationship between the resurrection of Christ and our preaching. The resurrection is not only the content of our preaching, but the very means of our preaching.

In the Gospel accounts of Easter, Jesus not only rises from the dead, but he also appears to his disciples, the very disciples who have forsaken and betrayed him. He not only appears before his disciples, but he speaks to them. For instance, in John 20, Mary Magdalene goes to the tomb while it is still dark on Easter morning, she looks in, and Mary *sees*. What she sees is that not only have they tortured Jesus to death on the cross, but that in one final indignity, someone has stolen his body. Even when the Risen Christ stands before Mary, she does not see and understand who he is. It is only when Jesus *speaks* to her, calling her by name, "Mary!" that she sees and believes.

Then, in the next Easter scene, Jesus appears to his disciples who have gathered behind locked doors. Thomas has said that unless he touches the very wounds of Jesus he will not believe. But then the Risen Christ tells Thomas to touch his wounds and believe. At that point Thomas says, "My Lord and my God." We are not told that Thomas took Jesus up on his offer and actually touched his wounds. It was enough simply for Jesus to *speak* to Thomas, and then Thomas believed. The Risen Christ is one who comes to his disciples and resumes the conversation that has been so cruelly ended by the cross. He speaks to them, he addresses them, and he calls them by name. This is the bedrock of Easter faith—the speaking of Christ.

But an additional claim is being made here. Easter is not only those series of events whereby the Risen Christ speaks to his disciples, but Easter is also the engine that sets in motion the preaching of his disciples. In Acts 2, at Pentecost, Peter preaches. It is astounding that this is Peter who preaches. Remember where we left Peter in the darkness on Good Friday morning? Even though he has said that he would stand up for Jesus, Peter failed. When confronted by that maid in the courtyard in the Gospel of Luke, Peter cannot summon the strength to say anything. He denies Jesus three times. But now, when facing off with a mocking mob in Acts 2, Peter comes out and preaches. He preaches an effective sermon that leads the entire congregation to ask, "What do we have to do to be saved?"

Something very strange and powerful must have happened between the death of Christ and this scene in Acts 2. What has happened is the resurrection. And that resurrection empowers even a cowardly betrayer like Peter to preach. Easter is not only the content of our proclamation, but the means of our proclamation.

Thus you can understand why the German theologian Willi Marxsen could claim that Jesus rose into preaching. It is as if Jesus rose into our proclamation and lives in our preaching. And the theologian Bultmann claimed that, "The Risen Christ meets us in preaching as nowhere else." That might be too strong a claim to make, but it is good for us preachers to be reminded that the Risen Christ speaks to us, and that is how we are able to speak.

In fact, when it gets down to it, this is about the only solid evidence I have for the resurrection—the fact that over 2,000 years later we are still preaching the resurrected Christ, and people are still hearing. Every time, in your church or mine, when somebody hears and believes it is like Easter all over again. It's a miracle, a miracle no less than the miracle of the Risen Christ himself.

Forgive me for telling, and tirelessly retelling, instances of when people, even in my preaching, *hear*. I love those stories of the person who emerges from our church and says, "Your sermon really spoke to me today. I have really been addressed by what you have said. My life has been changed in your preaching." I take such declaration to be, not so much an affirmation of my good preaching, but an affirmation of Easter. The Risen Christ is loose, he is speaking, speaking to some of the same ones who have betrayed and forsaken him. It's a miracle.

Do we really want to be part of such a miracle? Oh, I will tell you that the thing I don't like about preaching is when the people don't listen, they don't hear, and they don't respond. But just let one of them hear, undeniably, really hear, and what is my reaction? Fear. It is a fearful thing to fall into the hands of the living God. It is a fearful thing to have my pitiful words commandeered by the Risen Christ, used to speak to someone, to call someone by name. I can deal with failure in preaching, but success?

There is something about me that really needs to believe that preaching is ineffective, that people don't really believe. That way I don't have to worry so much about my preaching. I don't have to assume responsibility for my preaching. I can throw a few spiritual ideas at them on Sunday and let it go at that. But what if people actually hear? What if the Risen Christ continues to speak, and primarily through preaching?

The reformers said that, "The preached Word of God is the Word of God." That is an awesome claim for preaching. Are you up for it?

The great theologian Karl Barth said that anytime anybody hears something in the reading of Scripture or in the preaching of the Word, it is a miracle, a miracle quite close to the same miracle that we witness in Genesis 1. Once, there was nothing but dark, swirling, formless void and chaos. And then, "God said . . ." God said let there be light, and there was. Let there be a world, and there was.

I look at my pitiful sermons, my jumble of words, and my collection of notes. Not much there. But luckily, after Easter there is the presence of a living God. There is death, defeat, and silence. But then, "And God said . . ." And there is life.

Every preacher knows this. We've all had those experiences of working as hard as we know how on a sermon, and it is obvious that the people hear nothing. We've got a dozen explanations for that. But we also have had—even the most mediocre of us preachers—that experience of not doing our very best in the sermon and yet after the sermon, someone reports that he or she has really heard something. I have no explanation for that sort of miraculous hearing except that Easter is true. Christ is risen from the dead and he has spoken, and he continues to speak, even to those who betrayed him.

All preaching is based on the miraculous affirmation, "Christ is Risen! He is Risen Indeed! Alleluia!"

When Preaching Is Out of Control

I'll admit it. I like to be in control. I don't think of myself as a "control freak." However, I want there to be a minimum of chaos. On Sunday, for instance, I like to have a general idea of where we are going to be by noon. It is fine for the Holy Spirit to be invited into our worship, but only to a degree. I like the Holy Spirit to have some room for movement, but not all that much.

I believe it is helpful in the planning process to state a theme of where the sermon might go on a Sunday like this one, with a text like the one assigned. After all, we ought to know where we are going, and if we don't, we'll never get there. However, the statement of theme might be guilty of giving the illusion that we have somehow, by simply stating a theme or a message for the day, controlled where we are going. Most preachers learn very early that preaching is not an easily controlled activity. And I like to be in control.

Some time ago Barbara Brown Taylor stated that "something happens between the preacher's lips and the congregation's ears that is beyond prediction or explanation." Taylor notes an experience that every preacher has, sooner or later: "later in the week, someone quotes part of my sermon back to me . . . only I never said it. There is more going on here than anyone can say."[1] And how! In order to prepare our sermons well, we need a fairly clear idea of our intentions. But as Eugene Lowry comments, in preaching there can be a huge gap between intention and result.[2]

And so a distinguished literary critic, in pointing out the great gaps that occur in literature between a writer's intention and the results that take place in the reader, calls his book *The Uses of Misunderstanding*. How well I recall interviewing an older preacher, asking what he had learned

1. Taylor, *The Preaching Life*, 85.
2. Lowry, *The Sermon*, 35.

in forty years of preaching. He answered, "The possibilities for misunderstanding are virtually limitless." And how!

How many times have you stood at the door, on a Sunday morning, and a layperson says to you, "That was a great sermon on . . ." And you want to say, "But I never said that. That was not what this sermon was about." Too late. The sermon is already out of your hands and into the congregation. Something has wrenched the sermon from your control. The sermon is not, therefore, best conceived of as a skillful packaging of ideas that are delivered to a congregation. Rather, a sermon is an event, a conversation between pastor and people that can go in almost any direction.

I remember an educational theorist years ago telling teachers, "Teaching is not telling and listening is not learning." This teacher of teachers had learned that education is a more indeterminate, risky endeavor than simply delivering information. The receiver is busy intruding powerfully on the message that is delivered. We cannot predict where a sermon will finally go. Rather than predicting, we ought to consider that perhaps the most important preaching task is offering, intending to evoke an event, but not being able to control that event. My friend Eugene Lowry likes to say that the preacher's work is to help people get to the point where they can perceive what God is doing and open themselves to that. Beyond that, preaching is mostly out of our control.

We are not simply delivering a package of information to a congregation. In the sermon, we are walking a journey together, engaging in a conversation. In any conversation, there must be a willingness on the part of each partner to be changed through the conversation. A lecture is one-way communication. The speaker hopes to change the listeners. But in a conversation, all of the speakers are also listeners. As you preach, you are busy listening to the congregation, picking up on a number of subtle, but powerful cues from them that tell you how you are communicating. The congregation is also struggling to hear what you are saying. But as they struggle, they are also busy rearranging what they hear.

Add to this the Holy Spirit. By God's grace, the Holy Spirit takes our pitiful words of preaching and enlivens them, rearranges them, helps them to catch fire in people's lives.

In the African American tradition there is the powerful use of silence. The preacher stops frequently throughout the sermon, sometimes even in mid-sentence, to let the congregation have some room to process what is being said. This is crucial space. Not only does it provide space for people to thoughtfully consider what is being said, to catch up with the flow of ideas, but it also provides for the Holy Spirit to come. It is in the gaps, these life-giving spaces, that the Spirit can roam, can take hold of lives, and can make of our preaching more than it would be if left up to us. No one did this better than the great Howard Thurman of Marsh Chapel, Boston University. The phrase "pregnant pause" was meant for Thurman's preaching.

Eugene Lowry says, "We cannot control the result of our sermon. We do our best, of course, but know that with God's Word we are at best working provisionally. The Spirit works with certainty. Our task is to try to maximize the possibility of proclamation happening. We simply cannot produce it by will."[3] And I like to be in control.

Better than seeing the sermon as my product, I ought to see it as my gift, my part in the divine-human conversation that takes place in the congregation. I ought to enjoy the freedom that is given in the sermon, the freedom for new insight to arise in the congregation, the freedom for the Holy Spirit to take my poor sermon and make it mean even more than I intended. There can be great grace in learning to enjoy being out of control in the sermon!

3. Lowry, *The Sermon*, 28.

Preaching as Oral Communication

We make a weird move in our seminary homiletics classes. After having spent at least sixteen years educating these students out of their natural, oral culture of stories, images, jokes, and slang, and into a literate world of books, term papers, and abstract ideas, in one semester of a preaching class we try to drag them back to their oral talents.

Yet many commentators have been saying for some time that our entire culture is making the same move. Gutenberg helped to create the modern world with his printing press, a world in which the written, printed word predominated. Now many believe we are in the "postmodern" world where TV, computers, and other technologies have dismantled the literate culture and returned us to oral communication. Most of us receive most of our information through TV. Even a hip newspaper like *USA Today* tries to look like TV. The words on my computer screen may look like print, but what looks like type are only flashes of light, having more in common with the transience of the spoken word than the permanence of print.

Preaching must recover a sense of itself as an oral event. When, in your first preaching class in seminary, the professor said, "You will hand in three sermons this semester," those weren't sermons. Nothing lying on paper is a sermon. A sermon must be spoken, "done," performed. You haven't "done" King Lear if you read it. It's a play; therefore it can only be encountered in performance. Sermons are like that.

Therefore Clyde Fant, great teacher of preachers, spoke of the need for "oral preparation" of sermons. Fant advised us first to speak a sermon; then, only after we have tried speaking the sermon aloud in our study should we put anything down on paper. On paper, the eye gives clues to the reader through paragraphs, underlining, punctuation. The hearer has no such clues; therefore the speaker must help the hearer with transitions, emphases, and coherence. A manuscript can delude us into thinking that our sermon is more coherent and comprehensible than it really is when spoken.

Retaining a sense of orality is perhaps the greatest advantage of preaching without a manuscript. A sermon manuscript gives us preachers the illusion that we have "done" a sermon when at last we have fixed words on a page. On the page, the reader is given clues by the writer when to pause, when to stop and ponder, when to move on. When spoken, the sermon has no punctuation marks, no paragraph indentations, none of these printed clues to help it communicate. In writing out our sermons, our sentences tend to be too long, our thought patterns too involved. We lose a sense of movement and rhythm.

Even when we know our manuscript well, we tend to look at the manuscript rather than look at our listeners. We miss clues that our listeners are sending us when they don't understand, or when they are losing interest. Preaching is a visual as well as an auditory affair. Oral communication requires eye contact as sender and receiver send one another clues about what is being communicated.

Most of us preachers must work to regain and to develop our oral skills. In some traditions, such as the Pentecostal, or in African American churches, preachers never lose those skills. TV's presentation of a composed, polished talking head, eyes fixed on the viewer (reading from the teleprompter!) gives us preachers some competition. Yet, oral skills are learned—eye contact, timing, pacing, voice control, memory, humor, posture are all skills that we can improve despite our innate gifts or lack thereof.

Have yourself videotaped. Ask yourself, in viewing this tape, "How do I appear to others as I speak?" Listen to the audiotapes or videotapes of other preachers, even attempting to imitate some of their oral techniques. Imitation can be the path toward eventually finding your own voice. Preachers have learned much from Garrison Keillor.

Deliver your sermon in front of a mirror.

I find myself watching the performers on *The Comedy Channel* on our cable TV. Despite the content, here are people who speak for a living, who develop their sense of timing, their interaction with the listeners, their love of words for the sheer sound of them.

And give yourself credit. I have noted how even the most mediocre of us preachers demonstrate a facility with the spoken word, skill in oral communication, the holiness of one human being telling the truth to others, which is rare in our culture.

So, if we are moving from a once predominately print and literate culture to an oral and imaged culture, we preachers may be rediscovered. Our day has come!

The Art of Preaching

A number of years ago a distinguished homiletics professor wrote a book on the science of preaching. He noted those insights, techniques, and methods that are required to preach well. His book was a massive exercise in the explication of the precise steps on the way to a good sermon.

This sort of thing flies in the face of what I believe about the preaching task. From my experience with preaching, I believe that preaching is much more of an art than a science. Learning to preach is more akin to learning to paint in watercolors than it is to learning to mix chemicals together to produce a predictable chemical reaction.

As one of the most demanding and difficult of pastoral tasks, preaching requires so wide a range of gifts and skills. It is no wonder that some have asked if it can be taught at all. "Preachers are born, not made." While natural gifts of the preacher count for much, good preaching is an art, not magic. It must be learned. As with any art, preaching is an alloy of gifts and training, natural inclination and cultivated dispositions.

Because preaching is an art, the best methods of homiletical education tend to be modes of apprenticeship—a novice looking over the shoulder of an experienced master of the art in order to get the insights, moves, and gestures required to practice that art. For this reason, homiletics is often the most difficult practice to teach at a seminary, and often the most poorly learned. Preachers are made through intense engagement between a master and a novice, the master being willing to take the time to get to know the novice, the novice being willing to submit to the moves, habits, and insights of the master. Preaching cannot be learned, as it is often attempted to be taught, with a group of twenty passive seminarians sitting through lectures in a homiletics class, handing in a few written "sermons" during the course of the semester.

Chrysostom says that a preacher needs two basic attributes: "contempt of praise" and "force of eloquence." I find it fascinating that he links these two particular qualities. If the preacher lacks eloquence, then the preacher "will be despised by the people and get no advantage from his sublimity." On the other hand, if the preacher "is a slave to the sound of applause," the preacher will speak more "for the praise than the profit" of the congregation.[1] Art will subsume theology and verbal dexterity will be more important than biblical interpretation. Thus, while the great Chrysostom does not shrink from calling for artful eloquence in preaching, it is always art in service to gospel truth.

There has always been a certain uneasiness among Christian preachers in admitting that preaching is an art, a craft with certain techniques and skills that can be learned and refined in the practice of preaching. If preaching is a gift of God, an act of revelation, does it not seem disingenuous of a preacher to prepare, plan, craft, and practice the delivery of a speech that ought to come straight from God? Paul shows this tension when he tells the church at Corinth,

> When I came to you, brethren, I did not come proclaiming to you the testimony of God in lofty words or wisdom. For I decided to know nothing among you except Jesus Christ, and him crucified. And I came to you in weakness and in fear and much trembling. My speech and my proclamation were not with plausible words of wisdom, but with a demonstration of the Spirit and of power, so that your faith might rest not on human wisdom but on the power of God (1 Cor 2:1–5).

It is noteworthy that Paul says that he "decided"—that is, planned and contrived—to speak in a certain way to the Corinthians. He consciously constructed his appeal to them in order that it not appear self-consciously constructed, so that the Corinthians might not be impressed by Paul's oratory, but rather by the "power of God." In other words, there is no way around the necessity of rhetoric: consciously or subconsciously contrived ways of speaking that aim to persuade listeners. Paul is a great model for us preachers as we marvel at the wide array of creative rhetorical devices that he employs in order to communicate his beloved gospel. It is a privilege to be engaged with you in better biblical preaching.

---

1. John Chrysostom, *Six Books on the Priesthood*, 5.1–8 (p. 127).

Being Present in Our Preaching

"You were really present to us in your sermon today, preacher," he said on his way out of church last Sunday. What did he mean by that? Are there Sundays when I am absent?

I suppose that his remark was an affirmation that this sermon really seemed to mean something to me. I was "there" in a way that was noticeable and engaging. Perhaps that is not a bad distinction between a sermon and a lecture. A lecture is usually a rather "cool" presentation. A few ideas are put out on the table for reflection, consideration, and possible adoption. The ideas may mean something to the lecturer or they may not.

On the other hand, in a sermon, there is the expectation that the preacher will be "present." The moves made within the sermon must not simply be general ideas that may or may not have any relevance to the preacher. They must be ideas that, to some degree, the preacher is trying to embody in his or her life. The effective sermon is not simply a report on what the preacher may or may not think. Rather, the engaging sermon engages the hearers, it takes them somewhere they would not go without the power of the sermon. It makes a claim upon the hearers. They understand themselves to be addressed, summoned because it is clear that the preacher has also been addressed, summoned by the very word the preacher is attempting to preach.

Sometimes some preachers are accused of being "manipulative." Verbal manipulation can be a problem. However, we preachers ought to acknowledge that every one of our sermons is a sermon about matters that deeply concern us. We really do want to persuade our hearers, want to change them, want to encourage them to internalize these ideas in their lives.

The gospel of Jesus Christ is not merely some report on an interesting philosophy. Rather, the gospel is a matter of God's action and human response. The gospel is a claim about the mighty acts of God and therefore that claim must be an act, a summons, a deed.

Detachment can be the death of preaching. In fact, for the preacher to be detached from the subject matter is a basic violation of what the gospel is all about and therefore what preaching is all about.

How can we preach in such a way that it is obvious we are present in our preaching? Some of the advice your English composition teacher gave you in high school is relevant. It is better to speak in the present tense than in the past tense when using verbs. The active voice (she knows that . . .) is better than the passive voice (she had known that . . .). Simple, direct sentences are to be favored over complex sentences. Short, uncomplicated sentences convey energy and directness. As someone has said, the passive voice is always about something that took place somewhere else other than here and at another time other than now.

Concrete details are much better than abstract generalizations. I remember hearing about a teacher of preachers who asked students in his homiletics classes to call out all of the big theological words they had learned in their seminary classes, words like redemption, atonement, sanctification. Then he asked them to think of one everyday noun that could stand for and exemplify those big words, words like bread, water, wine, birth. He was trying to get his budding preachers to move from the detached abstraction engendered by the seminary studies to specific engagement. What are our sacraments if not concrete embodiments of matter, which without the bread or the wine would remain theological abstractions? Preaching that is present is therefore preaching that is sacramental.

If something is universally true, it is best grasped through the particulars of life. Things that are generic and abstracted tend to float above human experience. You will note that Jesus is a model for us in this matter of concrete communication. Jesus spoke of coins, seeds, soil, and the stuff of everyday life to speak of divine matters.

Avoid standing off from the sermon or from yourself in the manner in which you speak about the sermon. Don't refer to the sermon or to yourself as preacher, or to the listeners as listeners. Why say things like, "This morning I would like to have you consider the possibility that . . ."? Instead, just begin by saying, "Let's look at the problem of . . ."

Lately I've become annoyed at the way we preachers will speak about something called "the Christian community," when what I suppose we are talking about is church.

Don't talk about a story, or report on a story, or explain it. Tell the story. Rather than introduce a story with something like, "There is an old story that I heard some years ago, I have forgotten just where, perhaps you have heard it, which I would now like to retell again to you." Rather, simply begin, "One day there was a little girl who did not know which way to turn in a dark wood . . ."

Rather than summarize conversations between people, "One day Jesus was met by an interesting man who had some interesting things to say to him," say, "'What have I got to do to inherit eternal life?' he said to Jesus." It is always better to show than to report. If the conversation is interesting, don't tell your hearers that it is interesting. Rather, repeat the conversation for them and, if it is interesting, they will know it without your telling them.

Study the art of storytelling. Storytellers seem to involve their listeners in the action of the plot, seek to have their hearers identify with the various characters in the story. Isn't that what we want them to do with the gospel?

Extended quotations, even if they are from Scripture, get to be tedious and difficult to follow. Again, in quoting, we are distancing ourselves from the material we are presenting. Our hearers likewise will feel distanced by the use of long quotations.

Generally, I think it is a good rule to avoid heavy-sounding theological abstractions. Use words like redemption, or atonement, or incarnation, which are all good theological words, and watch a congregation's eyes glaze over. All of these words speak of concrete, available experiences of God's ways with us. Talk about those ways, the primary theological encounter, rather than the abstracted theological report of that encounter, and you will be "present" in the sermon.

Perhaps above all, we must be interested in what we have to say, convinced that what we have to say is of singular importance for our hearers. I sometimes tell my students to search the biblical texts for the given Sunday and find something within the text that engages them. If they can't find something that engages them, they will never engage their congregations.

It is well for our hearers to ask us to be present in our sermons, interesting, engaging, and enthusiastic about the message we deliver. To be anything less is to raise questions about the validity of the message we have to deliver. The message we have been given is good news, the words of God unto life. Let us give that message with all of the clarity and all of the presence we can muster.

Play It Again, Sam

About the most damning thing one can say about another person's work in academia is, "This book says nothing new." In academia, when one says, "This book tells the truth, but unfortunately it tells us nothing new," that is the end of that.

Years ago, the great anthropologist Margaret Mead called us North Americans "Neophiles"—lovers of the new. We are infatuated with the new and improved model of everything. If something is new, we automatically assume that it is improved.

When our son was young, six or eight years old, I remember him protesting our taking him to church saying, "I've already heard the stories once. Why do I have to hear them again?" I assured him that, as a Christian, he could expect to hear these stories many times over. Christians never seem to tire of telling and retelling the same stories.

When one thinks about our lust for the new and the novel from the standpoint of Christian doctrine, it is an odd point of view. For most of the church's life, innovation had to fight for itself. Heresy was, by definition, new teaching. Most of the great minds of the church labored, in each age, to understand the tradition of the church, not in order to say something new, but in order to, in their own age, restate what is old in a way that cannot only be comprehensible to the contemporary age, but that is also faithful to the tradition.

Sometimes we preachers get trapped in a desire to say something new. You want to say what you say to your congregation in a new way. This can be a worthy goal, but taken too far it can become a fixation that obscures specifically Christian, specifically biblical truth.

I confess that I often fall into this trap. After all, I have been preaching now for nearly thirty years. So often when I come to an assigned biblical text, I say to myself, "Here we go again. One more time with the text that

I have preached dozens of times." Forgive me for longing for something new. "Today I want to preach to you on the parable of the prodigal son, this time from the perspective of the fatted calf."

We need to rediscover the truth that part of the power of preaching is its ability to restate what is known, lovingly to cherish what is loved in the faith of the church. My colleague Richard Lischer, in his fine book on the preaching of Martin Luther King Jr., *The Preacher King*, notes that in African American preaching, one of the tasks that the preacher fulfills is that of reminding the congregation what it already knows, telling the story once again in a way that the congregation recognizes the story as their beloved story.

During a sermon, after Martin Luther King has wandered around, invoking a number of contemporary scholars, stating some impressive ideas that he has learned in his study in seminary, he moves back to the biblical text, retelling the story of David and Goliath. The moment that he begins the story, one can feel (this was on a cassette tape) the congregation recognize the story. The congregation realizes that it is at last on familiar terrain. Someone in the congregation shouts, "All right now! Go ahead and tell it! Tell it!"

This is a glorious, holy moment in preaching, when the congregation remembers its story, the story that has nurtured it through thick and thin, the story that convenes us in the first place. Remembering the story has a way of "re-remembering" the congregation. Remembering our story, the congregation re-congregates around its central images.

Martin Copenhaver called my attention to a wonderful place in the book of Acts, at Antioch, where the apostle Paul received what Copenhaver says is perhaps the greatest compliment ever received by a preacher in the history of the church. After Paul finishes preaching a wonderful sermon, the congregation says, "Would you come back tomorrow and preach that sermon again?" (Acts 12:42).

What a compliment! I wish I could say I had received such a compliment. Preach that same sermon again!

What was the sermon that Paul preached which evoked this marvelous and flattering request? We look in Acts and we find out that Paul, in his sermon, certainly did not say anything new. Rather, he retold the beloved story of Israel. He recounted for Israel's children the history of the loving purposes of God with Israel, God's faithfulness despite Israel's infidelity. He told them what they already knew. He reminded them what they already knew. He reminded them of what they already believed.

We live in a culture in which there are many stories, many of them contradictory or counter to the gospel. Therefore we meet together on a regular basis to remember, to recall, to recollect.

How many times did Russell Conwell preach his famous "Acres of Diamonds" sermon? Something like five thousand times, as I recall. I have heard Tony Campolo preach his "It's Friday, but Sunday's Comin'" sermon on at least three occasions, and it was always a delight. In fact, it seemed an even greater delight to those of us who had heard it before.

At times, preaching takes us into new and unexplored territory. At times, preaching helps us to see new things, to explore new ways of thinking and feeling. But at other times, preaching tells the old, old story again so that we nod in ascent. We recognize ourselves again within the story and are given heart.

Newness can be a trap. Lurching from one new idea to another can lead to superficiality. Like honey bees, flitting from flower to flower and never settling down anywhere, we fail to take root. We fail to live with anything long enough for it to sink in, to become part of us.

In the last chapter of his magisterial work on contemporary American art, *American Visions: The Epic History of Art in America*, Robert Hughes says that we Americans are incurable lovers of the new. Hughes feels that this love of the new both accounts for the genius and the superficiality of American Art:

> A central myth, not only of American art but of America itself, was that of newness: the perpetual renovation which, from the moment of Puritan arrival in the seventeenth century, stood as the promise of God's contract with a chosen people in the New World. . . . By 1900 the myth of newness, of perpetual progress, had been vastly fortified and confirmed by technology: Americans could make anything, solve any problem, produce a Niagara of inventions, and lead the world while doing so. So it was hardly surprising that soon after modern art arrived in America, the idea of the avant-garde, representing progress in the imaginative sphere, should have been welcomed, seized on, and eventually institutionalized to a degree unheard of in Europe. Americans, more than any other people, learned to believe that art progresses: that its value to human consciousness lay in renovation, seen as therapeutic in itself . . .[1]

1. Hughes, *American Visions*, 619–20.

In a transient, highly mobile society, people long for roots, something that endures. Those with responsibility for the church have, as one of our responsibilities, the loving nurture of the church's tradition. Each age must be enculturated into the narrative that has sustained the church through the ages. Each generation in the church ought to have the delight of rediscovering, within the wealth of the past, riches to sustain us in the present.

When our children were young, and we struggled with them within the Sunday service, there were those wonderful moments when at last, in the worship of the church, the church lifted up something, some act of worship, some prayer, or insight that the children knew. You could see their eyes light up. You could see their minds spring to attentiveness.

"I know that!" they seemed to exclaim.

We are the same. We love to be reminded of what we already know. We enjoy the opportunity of acknowledging the truth that is within us. We adore those moments when we hear the voice and delightedly recognize it to be the voice of the one who has loved us and is therefore loved by us.

Often the church is described as a place that is threatened by newness. True. Yet in our particular cultural context, that which is old and traditional may bear a threat. Let us not shy away from encounter with that threat.

SECTION 2

Special Issues in Preaching

Preaching as Entertainment?

Some years ago, social critic Neil Postman wrote an engaging book, *Amusing Ourselves to Death*. Postman's thesis was, in short, that we Americans are no longer interested in information, truth, or transformation. All we want is to be entertained. We have less interest in actually playing a sport than watching sports. We have become passive recipients of stimuli, sitting back and waiting to be entertained. Interestingly, toward the end of his book, Postman wondered about the effect of this entertainment culture, as he called it, upon the presentation of the Christian faith. Noting how much contemporary preachers utilize television, Postman wondered how the entertainment medium of television would attract Christianity. A communication medium is not neutral. The medium affects the messages. How could television, which is essentially passive, entertainment oriented, and integrally tied to consumerism, possibly be an adequate vehicle for the presentation of the Christian faith? Postman feared that in utilizing television, the Christian faith would be irreparably disfigured.

A number of years ago, when I was teaching homiletics in Germany, I showed my German seminarians videos of a group of American preachers. After viewing the videos, the German students were asked, "What do you think is the distinguishing characteristic of American preaching?"

They answered in unison, "Entertainment."

I was somewhat surprised by their characterization of American preaching. They ascribed it to the role of television. I resisted this characterization, but maybe they had something. A retired pastor told me that the main difference between when he entered the ministry sixty years ago and today was, "People came to church to learn and receive God's Word. The preacher had only the responsibilities to proclaim the Word obediently. The people's job was to listen. Today, the preacher is expected

to grab people's attention, to entertain them. If the preacher doesn't entertain, they go to another church."

In 1997, a study was done of student evaluations of their professors
at the University of California, Berkley. When the students praised their
professors, their highest praise included words like *humorous, fun, jokes,
entertaining*.

The Mills Corporation of Arlington, Virginia, has been transforming American shopping malls from centers for retail trade into places for
eating and entertainment, where shopping malls contain zoos, movie
theaters, amusement parks, and theme restaurants.

Of course, preaching as entertainment is not completely new. Billy
Sunday knew the value of a good show. But few of us took Billy Sunday
as our homiletical model. St. Augustine said that one of the purposes of
good preaching is to "delight." Surely delight is close to entertainment.
We preachers could wring our hands over this entertainment-dominated
culture. Or, we could capitulate into its grip. Flip your TV channels on
most any evening, and you will see preachers who have mastered the art
of preaching as television entertainment.

But perhaps there is another option for most of us. Few of us would
speak of the gospel, the good news of Jesus Christ, as entertaining. And
yet, the gospel at its best is certainly engaging. Perhaps the greatest sin
against the gospel of Jesus Christ is not to make it merely entertaining,
but to render it merely boring! Do not we preachers want to "grab" our
listeners? Perhaps the entertainment culture has merely raised the bar
for good preaching. Now, preachers must accept that we are going to be
judged in our speaking by comparison with the communicators whom
people watch on television.

I am sure that my own preaching has been affected by television,
even if unconsciously. Reading over sermons from fifty years ago, one
must be impressed by the rather leisurely pace. A preacher took time to
develop an idea, through a slow progression of ideas. Today, our sermons
are mostly fast-paced images. Not much time is spent on presentations
from one idea to the next. Rather, good preachers seek to render ideas
into concrete images.

Some time ago, the students where I preach accused me of preaching "MTV sermons." By that they meant that my sermons were mostly a
collection of various images, without much time spent on explanation or

explication. I realize, by their comments, that I have been affected by the media soup in which I speak.

I suppose the issue is not, "Will I be entertaining?" Rather, our chief concern should be *how*. I think the key to such judgments is the biblical text. How does the Bible deliver the truth that is within a given text? Most of my sermons are not nearly as resourceful or artistic as the Scripture itself. The Bible uses a wide array of artistic devices—humor, poetry, genealogy, story, invective, song—to convey a variety of messages. The key thing is the message. Entertainment in the service of the message is no sin. The greatest sin is to make the gospel conventional, expected, and uninteresting.

We all long to be entertained. That can be taken in a purely negative way as a plea for passivity, disengagement, and transformation of life into a spectator sport. Or it can be taken more positively. We all long to be delighted. We all long for those moments when we say, "This is interesting." Or perhaps when we say, "I have never heard it expressed that way before!" One of the reasons people come to church is to find meaning in their lives. To have their lives narrated in the light of the gospel. When that happens, they are struck with feelings close to something that could be described as entertainment.

Mere entertainment can never be the sole criterion for a sermon. However, we preachers are forced to evaluate our own composition and delivery of sermons, the effect of our personality on our listeners, the congregational context, and a host of other factors on how well they engage our listeners.

Thus, we preachers could receive many more troubling responses from our listeners than, "That was an entertaining sermon today, Preacher."

Topical Preaching—Again?

For the great majority of my ministry I have been in rebellion against a mode of preaching that was once quite popular in American pulpits, but fell out of fashion in the later part of this century—the topical sermon.

In the typical topical sermon, the preacher begins, not with the biblical text, but rather with a problem, some topic of contemporary concern. The topical sermon begins with our questions, with our problems, with an opinion about our current situation. Then it moves to interpret that question, that problem, or that situation in the light of the gospel.

As I was entering the preaching ministry, the topical sermon had been under assault for some time and the lectionary was beginning to be used within my denomination as a resource for preaching. Critics castigated topical sermons for their theological shallowness, their lack of biblical content, and their superficial readings of the contemporary situation. In the hands of someone like Harry Emerson Fosdick, extensively researched, theologically informed, eloquently stated, the topical sermon could be great. In the hands of most of the rest of us, the topical sermon was less than wonderful.

The lectionary offered us a way out of the predictable catalog of human ills and dilemmas that characterized topical preaching. Rather than beginning with our contemporary assessment of the human situation, the lectionary encouraged us to begin with the text, with a peculiarly biblical approach to biblically defined problems. Using the lectionary, we preachers did not have to thrash about, desperately trying to come up with some topic worthy of a sermon; the lectionary laid upon us our agenda. The lectionary helped us focus on manageable portions of Scripture, letting Scripture speak with its own integrity. We thus had the possibility of saying something that could not be heard from "Dear Abby," or on *60 Minutes*.

Surely, the basing of sermons upon the lectionary is partly responsible for the phenomenal success of homiletical aids such as *Pulpit Resource*.

Too many topical sermons offer conventional solutions to human problems rather than peculiarly Christian solutions. True, the Bible does not address all contemporary human questions, but perhaps the Bible wants to rearrange our questions, to entice us away from our merely contemporary infatuations, to take us places we would not have gone without the prodding of the Bible. Thus, many of us turned to the lectionary as a helpful discipline to keep our sermons yoked to Scripture.

And yet, I have come to see that we lectionary preachers need not exclude the topical sermon from our repertoire of homiletical forms. There are concerns that are worthy of a congregation's consideration that are not peculiarly biblical concerns—abortion, nuclear power, world order. Sometimes pastors become aware of certain needs and concerns within the congregation whose importance justify the text being used as a sort of springboard for consideration of those concerns.

I have found that congregations are much more willing to consider even the most conflicted and controversial subjects if they feel that the topic is placed before the congregation as a result of the pastor's attempt to be faithful to Scripture rather than as the result of the pastor's espousal of pet positions. Therefore, even lectionary preachers can, on occasion, become topical preachers.

For example, I recently heard a sermon that used the text Mark 10:2–6 as a springboard for a sermon on family life today. Mark 10:2–6 is not a text about many of the contemporary challenges to family life. For a variety of reasons, family life is not a major New Testament concern. Yet, it does seem fair to use Jesus' remarks about marriage and divorce in Mark as an invitation for your congregation to think about the Christian vocations of marriage and family.

How, in topical sermons like that one, when the preacher is clearly using a biblical text as a pretext for a sermon on a topic of interest to the preacher, can we avoid the pitfalls that have for so long plagued topical sermons? In his helpful book *Preaching the Topical Sermon*, Ronald J. Allen defends the use of the topical sermon and offers excellent guidance for preaching biblically responsible topical sermons.

I have adapted Allen's list of suggestions for preaching good topical sermons to my own list:

1.   Make a thorough examination of the preacher's own prejudices, opinions, and ideas about the topic under examination. Where are you in the topic that is being discussed? Why do you care about this topic at this time? By being aware of our preassociations and prejudices related to a given topic, we are better able to be critical of them and therefore more fair in our treatment of the topic.

2.   Thoroughly research the topic. List everything you need to know in order to be better informed about the topic. Credibility in the sermon will depend in great part on how convinced your hearers are of your own expertise to address this topic.

3.   Search for biblical perspectives on the topic. Note how different biblical writers may have different views of the subject. If the Bible is silent on the topic, admit that silence and honestly admit that your sermon will be based on authority other than biblical authority. Consider the possibility that, while the Bible may have material related to the topic, that material may be harmful to the discussion. In that case, a search of the ways in which the topic has been treated in the history of the church may be helpful. Does your denomination have a position on the topic under discussion?

4.   Estimate and assess your congregation's positions on the topic. What will be their points of resistance to what you say in the sermon? What are their probable questions about the topic? Are there recent congregational incidents or episodes in their life together that might be integrated into the sermon to help make this sermon their sermon? Picture in your mind various persons in the congregation and what it would be like for each of them to hear a sermon on this topic.

5.   State your own position on the topic. Your listeners want to know, finally, where you stand. If you have not yet made up your mind on the subject, let them know. By clearly stating your own position, in the early stages of the sermon process, you will help to give your sermon direction and coherence.

6.   Decide what you would like to accomplish in your congregation as a result of this sermon. Do you have some specific course of action to commend to them? Might there be opportunities for follow-up within the educational ministries of the congregation?

7. Design your sermon with all of these considerations in mind. Humor, personal testimony, and apt illustration can all be valuable tools in the art of persuasion. People are more attracted to someone's position when they feel that person is deeply committed and concerned about the topic.

Ultimately, a topical sermon must be judged by the same criteria as any other sermon. Is the message congruent with the witness of Scripture, the tradition of the church, the church's current struggle to be faithful? Some of the sermon examples at the end of Allen's book show, to my mind, many of the weaknesses as well as the strengths of topical preaching. It is very difficult to do justice to the peculiar, particular witness of the Christian faith when we are addressing important controversial issues of the day. Probably, topical preaching is no more prone to infidelity than expository, lectionary, or any other kind of preaching. Whatever the homiletical form, any preaching is a tough, risky business.

Proclaiming the Word with Children

I know that many of you will disagree with me when I say this, but nevertheless I'll say it: *Children's sermons are a drag.*

Don't get me wrong. I'm all for struggling to find ways to involve children in worship. Jesus has expressly placed children at the very center of his realm. In receiving children, we are receiving Jesus. The place of children in the church is not an optional matter for us Christians.

In my experience, the desire to have children's sermons in the congregation's worship comes from the sincere and laudable desire to include children in worship. We want to signal to our children that they are important. Unfortunately, I have my doubts that children's sermons are not the way to go.

I've sometimes said that I've got only two objections to children's sermons. They are not for children, and they are not sermons!

They are not for children—not for all of our children, at least. Most children's sermons are pitched to older elementary children alone. There is no way that younger children could make the connection between the rather complex analogies and the theological ideas. Young children do not develop abstract reasoning skills until age ten or twelve. Most of the congregation's children are being excluded from an activity that allegedly includes them all. The developmental differences between children can be vast. The cognitive abilities of a six-year-old are so different from those of a ten-year-old that communication with children in both age groups is very, very difficult.

They are not sermons. Few children's sermons are truly biblical. Most are insufferably moralistic, petty moral truisms rather than gospel. The gospel is thereby trivialized and sentimentalized. Invariably they urge children to be good, to act right, to do this or to do that, substituting law (albeit in sometimes charming ways) for gospel.

I recall the woman who was a child psychologist telling me, "I wouldn't mind children's sermons if they ever dealt with a subject of concern to children."

"Such as?" I asked. "Such as death, abandonment, the unfairness of adults, the injustice of the world." These were the subjects her child clients were intensely concerned with. Interesting, they are also the subjects of the Bible. Yet rarely are they the subject of children's sermons. Too often, the children's sermon implies that the gospel is little more than being good boys and girls.

A better way to include children than through (allegedly) children's sermons is through intentional attempts on our part to involve children in our sermons. Too often, the children's sermon has the effect of saying to the children, "We know that you are completely bored with everything that has gone on in this service and that you haven't the foggiest notion of what we are saying here, so we'll stop worship for a few condescendingly cute moments with you."

How do we know the children are not getting anything out of worship? Have you ever asked them? The sermon is only one aspect of Sunday worship. Even the sermon may be more accessible to them than we know. Daily, every child participates in many activities that have little immediate meaning to the child. The main meaning communicated may be something like, "Daddy and Mommy do many things, not because they are meaningful to you, but because they are deeply important to them." A sermon may be one of these things.

But we preachers can do more to reach out to children. In our illustrations, are they all about the dilemma of a middle-aged businessman? If so, we leave out a great many in our congregation. Few have been a great general or philosopher, but nearly everyone has been a new kid in the third grade, so frightened that you don't know what to do.

Children are not our only listeners who have difficulty following complicated, abstract arguments in our sermons. Many adults will appreciate it when our sermons become more concrete and less abstract, more narrative and less propositional, more specific and less general. My former colleague at Duke, John Westerhoff, often said, "If the worship excludes the children, change the worship."

While I may not be willing to go quite that far, I can see Westerhoff's point. Difficult-to-sing hymns and abstract, heavy concepts are not only a problem for children in the congregation. I recall the older man who told me, when I asked him why he had not been at church lately, that he did not come to church anymore because he could not sit for longer than fifteen minutes without having to go to the bathroom. I told him that he was not the only one in the congregation who needed to make frequent trips to the restroom! He could go there, every fifteen minutes, with most of our children.

Our children may make us more sensitive to a number of persons whom we are unintentionally excluding from some of our worship. Even when every sermon does not specifically include children, it is of relevance to others in the congregation. Christians learn that in the church we must serve others, and one way we serve others is by being patient in listening to sermons that, while not at the moment are helpful to us, are helpful to others.

Sermons may not be the best place for the church to reach out to its children. For children, actions speak much louder than words. The symbolic is more effective than the verbal. Children can participate fully in baptism and the Eucharist. They can use and hand out worship materials. They can sing and pray. Older children can read the Scripture on Sunday. We Protestants sometimes act as if worship through the word is the *only* worship. Especially in the case of children, act is primary to word.

As pastors, we are to serve the entire congregation in the name of the gospel. Do you know the names of all the children in your congregation? When children speak, do you listen? Our culture, in the words of Miriam Wright Edelman of the Children's Defense Fund, is none too friendly to children. Jesus gave these "little ones" an exalted place in his kingdom. Therefore, we pastors are being faithful to the gospel when we struggle with the issue of children in our worship. While children's sermons may not be the best or the only way to welcome our children in worship, we do well to struggle with the issue.

Delivery: How to Say What You Say

Ask a layperson to evaluate a sermon, and you will mostly hear a critique of the preacher's delivery. As one veteran sermon listener told me, "If it's read to you, it's a lecture. If it's spoken as if from the heart, it's a sermon." In our manner of delivery, the oral nature of a sermon is made apparent— or violated.

Unfortunately, we preachers are not always attentive to issues of delivery. Bad habits are often begun in seminary. The professor of homiletics says, "You will write three sermons for this class this semester." But those manuscripts, undelivered, are not yet "sermons." Better delivery is learned over a lifetime of preaching. The skills required for good oral communication are among the last to be acquired by us preachers. In preparing our sermons, sometimes we expend so much effort in devising what we say that we allow insufficient time and energy for how we say what we say.

Here are some principles I have found helpful in regard to issues of sermon delivery:

1. More or less memorize your sermon. This may involve no more than memorization of the basic outline or the various moves you want to make in the sermon. Memorization need not be word-for-word. In fact, it should not be. However, memorization will free you to move from worry over what to say to concern over how to say what you say.

2. The process of memorization will help you to be attuned to the flow and the images within the sermon. If you find a string of abstract concepts difficult to remember, how much greater will be the congregation's difficulty in following your sermon? Stories and images have a rhythm, a flow inherent within them.

3. As part of this process, speak your sermon aloud from start to finish in your study or while on a walk. If you repeatedly have difficulty remembering some point, this is probably a sign of some problem in the flow of the sermon. Besides, a sermon sounds quite different spoken aloud, resounding in your ears, than on Sunday morning when I say to myself, upon hearing myself recite a part of my sermon, "I can't say that!"

4. Practice before a mirror, if you can stand it. Attempt to be aware of your posture and gestures. What are you communicating to the congregation by your physical appearance?

5. Establish the habit of listening to past sermons on audiotape or videotape a few days after their delivery. Attempt to detach yourself from the sermon and to be a critical listener. Where were points missed due to poor timing, bad intonation, or enunciation? How was your eye contact? At what points did the sermon lose force or energy?

Many of the secrets of good sermon delivery are skills that can be learned. Concerns and practice related to techniques of delivery need not make our sermons appear contrived or forced. In fact, hard work on delivery usually enables us to speak in ways that appear fresh and extemporaneous. I vividly remember watching an interview with the comic Robin Williams, in which he described how he watched hours of old Jack Benny films and how he went over certain scenes in Marx Brothers' comedies dozens of times attempting to imitate the gestures and duplicate their moves down to their most minute turns of the head or twists of the hand.

What struck me was that I had always considered Williams a great master of spontaneous and improvisational humor. He is. But the foundation for Williams' "spontaneity" was his exacting, tireless observation and training. Spontaneous, extemporaneous delivery is a learned skill.

I am convinced that when the preacher is grasped by a message worth delivering, the preacher will find the means to deliver the message. When we preachers have been truly encountered by a word from the Lord, I am convinced that the Lord will give us the means to speak that word before God's people. Thus, what we say is, in the final analysis, the first step in finding how to say what we say.

Imitation as Essential for Preaching

Among all the essential ingredients for the growth of speakers, Cicero gave *imitatio*, imitation, great honor. In classical rhetoric, students spent their first decades of study memorizing and delivering the orations of the masters. Before the developing orator attempted anything of his own, he had to learn by heart the words and gestures of others.

My colleague Richard Lischer, in his marvelous book on the preaching of Martin Luther King Jr., *The Preacher King*, vividly illustrates the pivotal role of imitation in the development of the young preacher. Almost every Sunday afternoon, King gathered with two or three of his fellow seminarians at the home of a distinguished African American preacher where they would take turns delivering famous sermons from preachers of the past. Lischer shows how these memorized sermons formed essential aspects of King's homiletic. These sermons would reappear, in bits and pieces, as set pieces in his sermons throughout the rest of his career.

Don't you find these observations counter to the conventional wisdom about imitation that we have received? Most of us have gotten the distinct impression that imitation is not "the sincerest form of flattery" but rather a dishonest, cheap rip-off by an insecure and inept preacher who needs to stop slavishly copying the homiletical style of others and start finding his or her "own voice."

Trouble is, our "own voice" is a mélange of the models we have inculcated, the sounds and gestures of others whom we admire, the range of tone and stress in the voices of those who have moved us. My voice is the sum of all whom I have heard and whose voices I have made my own.

Furthermore, as we have seen, classical rhetoric honored *imitatio*. Classical rhetoricians knew that the best way to good communication is by sincere and careful inculcation, submission of ourselves to the disciplined delivery of a master.

A young child does not learn speech theory or the rules of grammar in order to speak. The child imitates the speech of parents and parrots what is heard. You have heard me say before that I believe preaching is an art rather than a science, a craft. We grow in our preaching by looking over the shoulders of others who are good at the craft. Believing that *imitatio* is a good thing, I enjoy listening to tapes, both video and audio, of sermons by others.

Recently I heard a distinguished jazz musician, who is also a professor at a nearby university, extol the importance of imitation for the development of a jazz musician. He told about how, as a young man, he spent hours listening to recordings of great jazz artists. He said something that surprised me. He said that his first stirrings into the music world were as a child when he listened to his father play the piano and then he would attempt to duplicate the sounds his father made on the piano, without knowing a note of music. This he called "uninformed imitation."

Later he went to music school and studied music theory and composition. Shortly thereafter, this budding jazz artist began what he calls his period of "informed imitation." Now, armed with theory, with a basic understanding of the theoretical structure behind the making of music, he was ready to listen, in an informed and sophisticated way, to the music of the masters. He had a better understanding of the artistic problems they were encountering, he could hear the strokes of genius in the composition, he detected their mistakes and their attempt to correct them. "Imitation is the single most important skill for someone who wants to play jazz," he said.

I hear analogies for us preachers. Informed imitation, that's our goal. We don't listen to the preaching of others so that we can be slavish imitators. We listen as fellow artists, as those who have learned enough about preaching to know competence when we hear it, to respect the ways in which more experienced practitioners of our craft can teach us. I don't believe we discover or become confident in our "own voice" until we first have listened, appreciated, criticized, inculcated, internalized, and risen above the voice of others. Imitation is an essential aspect of our development of good preaching.

Preaching on Stewardship

I was asked, "Would you come to Atlanta and say a word or two in behalf of stewardship?"

"I haven't heard of stewardship in years. Do you mean money?"

"Some people have known it by that name. We prefer also to think of it as time, talent, as well as a number of other attributes."

Stewardship is one of those words that a lot of people think they know, and yet they really don't know. It has many different aspects. Each fall, you may be asked in your congregation to say a word or two in behalf of stewardship.

"To whom much has been given, much will be required" (Luke 12:48), said Jesus, provoking a head-on collision with some of his society's most widely held and deeply cherished values. Jesus dares to speak of our lives, all that we are and all that we have, as gift. You and I are not conditioned to think like that. We live in a society ruled by something called the Constitution, in which our lives are seen as entitlements rather than as gifts.

In this sort of society, there is not much room for gift or gratitude. Thus, for Jesus to speak of our lives as something that we have been given sounds strange. Every gift entails a giver, certain responsibilities and obligations. When we have no sense of our lives as gifts, we have no sense of obligation. To those who have been given nothing, nothing is required.

I was recently in a dinnertime conversation with a group of people who were talking about the then-current debate over affirmative action. Most of the people at that table could be fairly described as "self-made men." Each of them had achieved much in life through hard work and earnest effort. I, therefore, expected them to have a uniformly negative view of affirmative action, the notion that the government ought to take measures that would enable some people to have a hand up, a first chance.

You can imagine my surprise when one of the older men in the group looked around and said, "Every person seated at this table has been the beneficiary of affirmative action. We didn't call it that, but we asked for help from someone who knew your father, or called up someone who owed your mother a favor. When I graduated from the University of North Carolina in the Depression, my daddy called me and told me not to take the trouble to come home because there was no work. He advised me to go to Raleigh. He told me to go to the office of a man whom he had once befriended and ask him if he would hire me. I did so, and the man was good enough to give me a job, out of respect for my father. That's affirmative action the old way. We called it looking for a favor from somebody who owed your father, or we called it the buddy system, or networking, but it is still affirmative action."

The person who said that had been a United States senator, governor of our state, and president of our university. I thought it rather amazing, and even wonderful, that in our society of allegedly self-made men and women, he could still see his own life as a gift, a hand up offered to him by others.

The poet Maya Angelou, speaking to our first-year students on the first day they arrived on campus, said to them: "You have been the beneficiaries of the best that this society has to offer. We have given you the best education we know how to give. We have told you all that we know. Now, you owe us something." And then Ms. Angelou quoted Jesus, "To whom much has been given, much will be required."

The idea of equality often denies history. We did not all arrive at this place in the same way. Each of us has a different past. For some of us, that past includes discrimination, depravation, and a host of other particular historical factors that mock the notion of equality.

Jesus challenges the Enlightenment notion of equality by noting that some are given more than others. And the ones who are given the most, have the most required. Yet we live in a society in which those who are given the least, in education, in family and parental upbringing, are the ones of whom the government demands the most. You must get training. You must get a job. You must fulfill these criteria, or we will not let you be eligible for "benefits."

Few of us pastors mention money as often as the Bible mentions it. Jesus makes repeated, stunning statements about finances. "Where your money is, your heart is," he said. That is a strong statement. If you want to look into the quality of a person's soul, look at that person's checkbook stubs.

I have sometimes preached sermons on the theme, "It's not the money that's the sin, it's the way we use the money. Money is not evil, rather the evil is not keeping money in its proper place." And yet, I can think of a number of stories Jesus told, which imply that money is not neutral. The poor are not the problem. The rich have a very big problem, and the poor are, regardless of why they are poor, the blessing of God.

So St. Ambrose spoke to the rich in his congregation telling them that they were guilty of "usurpation" in their riches, usurping that which ought to be God's. St. Jerome said in a sermon that a rich person is automatically the recipient of ill-gotten gain, which was ill-begotten either by him or his father. I don't know that I would be able to make such sweeping claims, but at a minimum we could say that, from Jesus' perspective, money is a big issue.

In my last congregation the number one family, pastoral care problem was money. This is a surprising thing to say since we were a blue-collar, inner-city congregation. Almost no one in that congregation was "rich" by our standards. However, we were, most of us, the first in our families to have a surplus of funds. This meant that we were among the first in our family to have to make definite choices about how we would spend our money. We had made enough money to get us beyond providing the basic necessities.

My single-parent mother did not have to agonize over whether or not to buy me a car when I earned my license to drive. It was not even in the realm of possibility. However, by the time I had children we had to make a conscious decision about whether or not to buy our children a car. I learned in my last congregation that it does not take a huge amount of money to ruin a child.

Our congregations could do a better job of helping us to make better choices about money. Many of us are showing that we do not have the skills or the values to make wise decisions about money. We act as if the acquisition of things, of materialism, is a neutral affair. The Bible would say that our souls are at stake in these transactions.

The good news is that there are lots of people, people within this very congregation, who are making conscious choices not to get on the materialistic treadmill.

In Mark 10, we watch as Jesus confronts a rich young man. In Mark 13, Jesus forces us to look at a poor widow who recklessly gave all she had. These offer us preachers the opportunity to preach on stewardship, on the way in which our lives and all that we have are gifts from God. Will we treat our lives as our possessions, our achievements, or can we come to view our lives as God's gifts? Will what we have be seen as an obligation to accumulate, to insulate, and to keep things for ourselves? Or will our possessions be seen as a wonderful opportunity to reach out to others?

During the tragic aftermath of the Heaven's Gate suicides in California, a group of us pastors were discussing the tragedy. We agreed that these people ended their lives for a false god and a false faith. How could anyone do such a thing? One of the pastors observed that, in the reports about Heaven's Gate, the news reporter seemed either outraged or bemused that someone in contemporary America would still die for religion. "A curious thing in my congregation is that almost nobody has given his or her life for religion. And yet, in the past year, I've had a half-dozen people either die or come near death with heart attacks, high blood pressure, and other diseases brought on by stress related to work. In our society, you are considered crazy if you give your life for your faith, but you are considered normal if you drop dead for a dollar!"

Think about it.

Preaching and Pastoral Care

Preaching's purpose is the proclamation of the word of God. Yet while we preach, we also care for the congregation. How often have I heard someone say of his or her pastor, "Our pastor isn't much of a preacher, but he is certainly a wonderful pastor." Rigid distinctions between the gentle pastor who empathetically cares for the flock and the bold prophet who speaks the truth are due more to modern stereotypes than to biblical portrayals of the servants of God. Paul, for instance, saw himself as a preacher (1 Cor 1:17) and as a caring nurse for fledgling Christians (1 Thess 2:7). First Timothy urges early church leaders to preach the word and to tend the flock (1 Tim 2:1—6:1). Most pastors have therefore agreed with Phillips Brooks who, in his *Lectures on Preaching*, said to those who thought it impossible to be both preacher and pastor, "I assure you, you are wrong."[1]

As the pastoral care movement gained momentum in American churches beginning in the early 1920s, many mainline Protestant pastors wholeheartedly embraced pastoral psychology as an aid in preaching. Harry Emerson Fosdick said that his great discovery as a young preacher was that a sermon begins

> with the real problems of the people. That was a sermon's specialty, which made it a sermon, not an essay or a lecture. Every sermon should have for its main business the head-on constructive meeting of some problem which was puzzling minds, burdening consciences, distracting lives, and no sermon which so met a real human difficulty, with light to throw on it and help to win a victory over it, could possibly be futile.[2]

1. Brooks, *Lectures on Preaching*, 76.
2. Fosdick, *The Living of These Days*, 94.

Fosdick went so far as to describe preaching as "counseling on a group scale," and made the personal problems of his listeners central to his "life-situation preaching."

Twentieth-century pastoral care took, as one of its assignments, the affirmation of the individual and developed techniques for empathetic, nonjudgmental listening. Preaching appeared to many practitioners of pastoral care as pastoral counseling's polar opposite. They criticized traditional preaching for its typically authoritarian, moralistic, biblically simplistic and judgmental approach to human problems.

Yet when, by the mid-twentieth century, American preachers were wholeheartedly embracing the insights of psychology and directing their sermons to the needs of people, critics charged these later day practitioners of "life-situation preaching" with forsaking the biblical text in their often facile use of psychological answers to problems that may be as much theological as psychological in nature. In a therapeutic, psychologized culture, as many claimed North America had become, preaching, which always tried to offer psychology-based pastoral care, was criticized for playing into the hands some of the most provincial, limited aspects of our radically subjectivized society. Karl Barth dismissed modern attempts to reduce preaching to psychological therapy. "Preaching is not intended to be simply a clearer and more adequate explanation of life than can be arrived at by other means. . . . The congregation is waiting for the meaning of life to be illumined by the light of God."[3]

Each area of pastoral work has its own inherent values and its own integrity. While preaching is not "pastoral care on a group scale" (Fosdick) and pastoral care is not psychotherapeutic preaching, the two distinct pastoral activities can mutually enrich one another. In our work, we pastors do not make rigid distinctions between the various modes of ministerial activity. Preaching is a public, corporate, traditioned and traditional, proclamation-oriented pastoral function. Pastoral counseling, while not limited to individuals, tends to be more personal, one-to-one, and problem oriented than preaching. In preaching, the pastor is not merely speaking to human problems, but is rather proclaiming the faith of the church whereby our problems are addressed in a peculiarly Christian way. In pastoral care, human problems are informed by the psychological

---

3. Barth, *The Preaching of the Gospel*, 53.

perspective in a personal, direct, and caring way, which can both enrich and challenge the theological and biblical perspective.

Pastoral care aids preaching by giving the preacher a respect for listeners in their individual struggles. In counseling troubled parishioners, preachers are with their people in intimate, personal, face-to-face encounters. The preacher who is also a pastor is therefore less likely to make sweeping, generalized, universal judgments about "the human condition." Before making pronouncements from on high about human problems, the pastor will see specific human faces, the lives of individual members of the congregation who are struggling with these problems. Thus pastoral care provides a necessary context for faithful preaching.

Pastoral care activities like pastoral counseling not only provide the preacher much information about the lives and struggles of parishioners, but also build rapport between the preacher and the people. In one-to-one or small-group counseling experiences, people have the opportunity to relate to their preacher in a personal way. Surely this dynamic was what Paul had in mind when he blended the preaching and the counseling ministry in saying, "So, being affectionately desirous of you, we were ready to share with you not only the gospel of God but also our own selves" (1 Thess 2:8). People make themselves available to pastors who have made themselves available to the people. People listen to preachers who demonstrate that they have listened to their people.

Preaching can enrich pastoral care. Recent critics of contemporary pastoral counseling have noted the need for pastoral care to make clear what is specifically Christian in its care. What is the difference between pastoral counseling and secular counseling? Preaching helps to identify the pastor as representative of the church and its witness. In preaching, human problems are named and contextualized as concerns related to discipleship and faithful witness, not just personal psychological dilemmas. In coming to a pastor with personal problems, people realize that they are also coming before a preacher who has a sacred responsibility, through ordination, to witness to the historic faith of the church, to urge parishioners to lay their lives alongside the story which is the gospel, not simply to be psychologically caring and sympathetic.

Preaching is also pre-counseling activity. Parishioners are present with their pastor in greater numbers, for a more extended and focused time in preaching than in any other pastoral function. A sermon might be the only contact many people in the congregation will have with the pastor. What impressions will the people receive from their preacher? Will the preacher be experienced as someone who is sufficiently open and empathetic to the discussion of tough, personal issues? Or is the preacher the sort of person who always has an easy answer to every problem on the tip of the tongue? Preaching can open the door for counseling. When a preacher tackles some tough subject in a sermon, listeners may learn that the preacher is willing to discuss this problem with them in a more personal, individualized setting. Therefore pastors ought intentionally to address certain personal issues in their sermons.

As important as the pastoral care of our people is, preaching is more important. Preaching places our care in its proper context, articulates the divine judgment and the divine grace whereby individual struggles are set within the framework of the continuing story of God's gracious dealings with God's people. Without the weekly demands of the preaching office, the pastor's care easily degenerates into mere care with little else to inform or to form that care than the latest psychotherapeutic trends. Without the weekly attendance upon the preached word, the individual's desire for care easily degenerates into merely narcissistic craving for personal affirmation bereft of repentance, forgiveness, or vocation. Thus preaching is pastoral care's criterion for fidelity, that abiding norm whereby our care is rendered truly pastoral care, explicitly Christian.

The Character of the Preacher

Quintillius defined good public speaking as a matter of "a good man speaking well." The messenger must be congruent with the message in order for the message to be received. This is particularly true when the message is the gospel of Christ, a message that not only demands to be spoken, but also performed, embodied in the lives of faithful disciples. We preachers need to hear again the platonic truth that good speaking involves a good person speaking well. Character, Aristotle's *ethos*, is a prerequisite for faithful preaching.

Not long ago, *The Christian Century* had a recap of the most significant religious news from the past year. One story was of a number of prominent priests, charged with sexual abuse of children. Another told about a major embezzlement case at a large church in the Midwest. Malfeasance at the National Council of Churches. clergy-laity trysts in Texas. We mainline clergy snickered when the news was of the sexual shenanigans of TV evangelists, but this was close to home, mainline liberals, and none of us laughed.

A friend of mine, an economist, was asked to serve on the board of a church charitable organization that helps children in need. His first days on the board were a sort of religious conversion experience for him, so inspired was he by the work of the organization, so impressed was he by the tremendous amount of need. But then he learned of the salaries, the real salaries of some of the clergy staff. He uncovered accounting irregularities. After prayerful consideration, he brought it to the attention of the directors and . . . he was dismissed from the board.

He told me, "I think clergy, because they tell themselves that they are doing the work of the Lord, are particularly susceptible to self-deceit. If you're feeding hungry children, none of the moral rules apply to you which apply to other mere mortals."

When we preachers go sniffing about for signs of moral ineptitude, we need look, alas, for signs of ethical disorientation, no farther than the pulpit.

My colleague, Stanley Hauerwas, was recently asked about the moral confusion of contemporary clergy. Hauerwas said something to the effect that, "You have these people who get out of seminary thinking that their job is to 'help people.' That's where the adultery begins."

What?

"So you have these clergy," he continued, "who have no better reason for being in ministry than to 'meet people's needs.' Little Johnny needs picking up after school. And Johnny's mother, since she is working, calls the pastor, who has nothing else better to do, and asks him to pick Johnny up. And the pastor thinks, 'Well, I'm here to help people.' So he goes and picks up little Johnny. Before long the pastor meets a parishioner who is lonely and needs love and then, when caught in the act of adultery, his defense is that he is an extremely caring pastor."

In a culture of omnivorous need, all-consuming narcissism, clergy who have no more compelling motive for their preaching than "meeting people's needs" are dangerous. Certainly, there are many possible sources of clerical moral ineptitude. We clergy have been encouraged to wallow in the same psychotherapeutic mire as our people: meeting our needs, looking out for number one, if it feels good do it, the relentless scanning and feeding of the ego.

I believe that a major source of homiletical renewal is clerical lives grasped by something greater than ourselves; namely, our vocation to speak and to enact the word of God among God's people. Clergy ethics has its basis in homiletics. Morality is not a matter of being unattached to any external determination, free to think and act on the basis of our personal feelings of what is right. Contrary to the beliefs of liberalism, morality comes as a gracious byproduct of being attached to something greater than ourselves, of being owned, claimed, commandeered for larger purposes.

I heard Walter Brueggemann say to a group of us preachers, "If you are a coward by nature, don't worry. You don't have to be courageous to be a preacher. All you have to do is to get down behind the text. You can say, 'This is not necessarily me saying this but I do think the text says it.'"

We can hunker down behind the text! Disjoined from service to the text, all I can do is to serve the congregational status quo, run pastoral errands for the world as it is rather than let God use me to create a new world. And that is no fun.

I must make clear in my preaching that I preach what I have been told to preach. I serve the text, not those who listen. I must thereby help my listeners recover the adventure of being those who are baptized to listen to the text, those who bear the burden and the blessing of bending our lives in conformity to the demands of Scripture. Morality is always a liturgical matter. Who is the God we worship?

One of the great fictions of our age is the notion of the person without a role, the idea that we are most fully moral when we have divested ourselves of all external claims upon us. The liberal self, detached from any history, any claim upon the self other than the claims one has personally chosen, does not exist. All of us are busy being determined by something. Even the claim that I am living only "for myself" is an externally imposed claim by contemporary American society. So the question is not, "Will I serve some purpose larger than myself?" for freedom from such determination is impossible. The question is, "Will the master whom I serve be true or false?"

Preachers are those who are fortunate enough to have our lives caught up in the demanding, never quite finished, wonderful adventure of helping the church to hear God's word. Aristotle taught that it was too much to expect ordinary people to be good. About the best one could do for ordinary folk was to teach them good habits. Of the three artistic forms of proof that Aristotle listed as available to the public speaker, *logos, pathos, and ethos*, Aristotle knew that *ethos*, the character of the speaker, "constitutes the most effective means of proof" (*Rhetoric*, I, ii). Every time we stand up to preach, our characters, as they have been formed by the habits required for preaching, prove to the church that it is possible to make very ordinary folk (like preachers) into saints. That is, it is possible even for people who are innate liars to speak the truth. It is possible for people who are cowards by nature to be so caught up in some project greater than themselves that, despite themselves, they are heroic. I think it was after tackling a particularly difficult preaching assignment that Paul was bold enough to say to the Philippians, "Imitate me, you have a worthy example in us" (Phil 3:17).

Humor among Preachers

David Buttrick, whom I have heard be very funny in sermons, warns preachers that, "If you are a naturally funny person, your problem will be control; if you are not a naturally funny person, do not try."[1] I find it sad that Buttrick is so opposed to sarcasm, saying it is "always a form of veiled hostility," when he is often so good at it. Yet one can grant the general validity of his warning on humor. As the ancient preacher said, there is a time for laughter (Eccl 3:4), yet rarely does that time come in our sermons.

Quintilian said that "there are no jests so insipid as those which parade the fact that they are intended to be witty."[2] Nothing smells worse in a speech than a dead joke. Say something intended to be funny at the beginning of a sermon that is greeted by the impassive silence of the congregation, watch the rest of the sermon die. No wonder humor is avoided by most of us.

Buttrick says don't even try humor if we're not born with it. This is a variation of the old "preachers are born, not made" argument. Granted, we may be given certain natural gifts toward humor, but cannot humor be learned like any other sermonic skill? In my own preaching, I have learned from the humor of others, if only as their invitation for me to give rein to my own inborn inclinations. Yet I recall hearing Robin Williams—who is thought to be a genius at improvisational, impromptu humor—speak of studying for hours the humor of George Burns, Jack Benny, and Laurel and Hardy. Then Williams spoke of practicing, memorizing in front of a mirror for hours, attempting to duplicate their exact moves. Perhaps, if humor is a virtue in speaking, we ought to train for it.

1. Buttrick, *Homiletic*, 146.
2. Quoted in Corbett, *Classical Rhetoric*, 307.

We preachers ought to begin by acknowledging that there are parts of Scripture that are funny, particularly when read aloud. When Jesus uses hyperbole and exaggeration—straining at a speck in someone else's eye while ignoring the beam in your own—he surely baptized humor as a possible means of faithful communication.

Writer Kathleen Norris discovered the humor even in St. Paul when she heard the epistles read aloud in a monastery:

> Oscar Wilde once described Paul's prose style as one of the principal arguments against Christianity—but hearing Paul read aloud in the monk's choir allowed me to take an unaccustomed pleasure in the complex play Paul makes of even his deepest theology. To hear the joke working its way through 1 Corinthians 1:21 is to get the point: "For since in the wisdom of God the world did not come to know God through wisdom, it was the will of God through the foolishness of the proclamation to save those who have faith." Hearing the passage read slowly one night at vespers, I suddenly grasped the exasperation there, and God's good humor, and it made me laugh.[3]

I know that lots of people think preachers are among the least humorous of persons. But sometimes the gospel itself makes us humorists. To experience the great gap between who God has called us to be and who we really are, to see ourselves with some humility, not as the proud, righteous people we wish we were but as the frail and foolish people we are, is to smile. We could weep over our foolish sinfulness, but laughter may be more gracious, more creative. Therefore, wherever there is the gospel, wherever there is serious consideration of the limits of human presumptions, there is also going to be humor.

Jokes don't really have a place in sermons. To tell a joke that is obviously set down in a sermon without any relationship to the thrust of the sermon, is to risk trivialization of the sermon.

Yet when the gospel, laid next to the human condition, produces humor, then I think it's fine to let that humor shine through in the sermon. Many of Jesus' parables tend to be close cousins of our jokes. Whenever anyone who is high and mighty is brought down low (the pompous banker who slips on the banana peel), then we laugh. And there is a great deal of that sort of movement in the gospel; therefore there will be a number of opportunities for humor in our sermons on the gospel. The most appro-

---

3. Norris, *The Cloister Walk*, 32–33.

priate humor in preaching is that which arises out of our confrontation by the gospel.

Why, even Richard Nixon, whose humor was mainly unintentional, could be amusing. Nixon once related, "The day after Jack Kennedy gave his moving Inaugural Address, I went up to him and said, 'You spoke some words today that I wish I had said,' and he said, 'I guess you mean the part about ask not what your country can do for you,' and I said, 'No, I mean the part about I do solemnly swear.'"[4]

His self-deprecation was a rare moment of Nixonian humanity. If Richard Nixon can be funny, so can you.

A priest approached Groucho Marx as he was having lunch and said, "I want to thank you for all the pleasure you've brought into life," and Groucho said, "And I want to thank you for all the pleasure you've taken out of it."

4. Dole, *Great Political Wit*, 50–51.

Preaching and the Text

How Unbiblical "Biblical Preaching" Can Be

It is a great challenge to be a biblical preacher. It isn't easy to be a biblical preacher because our culture has myriad ways of distracting us from the intrusive voice of God. Alien texts are forever trying to elbow out the biblical text for our attention. For what it's worth, the following are what I consider to be our most persistent contemporary abuses related to biblical preaching.

Psychology is God. In some of our preaching, you get the impression that Jesus is some sort of itinerant therapist who, for free, traveled about helping people to feel better. Ever since Fosdick, we mainline liberals have been bad about this. Start with some human problem like depression. Then rummage about in the Bible for a relevant answer. Problem is, we're starting with our current definitions of our problems. Maybe the Bible could care less about our problems, as we define them. Where did we get words like *depression, anxiety, self-esteem, felt needs*? Not from the Bible. In regard to depression, I can name you passages where the Bible appears to want to *provoke* depression rather than cure it! And my "felt needs," before I meet the Bible, are usually the result of sin rather than the path to salvation.

As one of my students put it, "Modern American people tend to have psychological problems because that's the only kind of problems we're permitted to have." A few years ago, a popular book called us "The Psychological Society." And we are. All human problems are reduced to psychological problems.

Now, Jesus really does care for and reach out to hurting people. However, the Bible doesn't want to "help people." It wants to help people *in the name of Christ*. Christ has a very different notion of our problems than we do. Any good that comes from our encounter with the Bible is not that it pumps up our self-esteem or it gives us three surefire steps to personal happiness. The good that comes to us from the Bible comes as a gracious byproduct of having been met by the Shepherd who is Jesus. The Bible doesn't just want to speak to us. It wants to change, convert, detoxify us.

Every time we let the world set our homiletical agenda, scaling down our speech to that which anybody off the street can hear and understand without conversion or training, we lose the battle before it begins. We concede too much territory to the enemy. The psychologization of the gospel—reducing salvation to self-esteem, sin to maladjustment, church to group therapy, and Jesus to Dear Abby—is our chief means of perverting the biblical text. Jesus is our Savior, not our therapist!

We gather on Sunday not just for comfort, but also for *truth*. If we are to get better in what ails us, if we are to grow, then the path must lead through the realm of honesty, confession, and truthfulness. Each Sunday we gather to plumb the depths of human consciousness, to attain an honesty that would be otherwise unavailable to us if we were left to our own devices.

Politics is God. Previously, we mainline, liberal Protestants were the ones who were so bent on mixing religion and politics. Now it's the Religious Right, but it's essentially the same project. It's a politicized project that is tough for biblical preachers; once they get infatuated with politics, they don't stay biblical for long.

Let's face it, the Bible is downright nasty toward folk in power, particularly if they work for the government. Remembering what Caesar did to Jesus, we tend to get nervous whenever Washington or Moscow is mentioned. Even when Paul tells us to obey Caesar's functionaries, it's more along the lines of, "Go ahead and obey these people because when Christ returns, he's going to give them what they deserve anyway." It isn't just that "power corrupts," it's that the gospel tends to be so prejudiced against our power and those who use it that the less said, the better.

The New Testament has virtually nothing to say to folk who enjoy a powerful majority, but everything to say to those who are a persecuted minority. I find little scriptural help for how to run a multi-million-dollar political action group, but lots of verses about what to do when you are in jail.

Last fall, as I was preparing in my office for the Sunday service, the telephone rang. "Who's preaching in Duke Chapel today?" asked a nasal,

Yankee-sounding voice. I cleared my throat and answered, "The Reverend Doctor William Willimon."

"Who's that?" asked the voice. "The Dean of the Chapel," I answered in sonorous tone.

"I hope he won't be preaching politics. I've had a rough week and I need to hear about God. My Baptist church is so eaten up with politics, I've got to hear a sermon!"

I think we must train our congregations to listen to our sermons, not merely asking themselves questions like, "What does this have to do with me?" or "How can I use this message in my work tomorrow morning?" Rather, we all must discipline ourselves to ask, "Where is God meeting us in this text today?" We must work under the hermeneutical assumption that the Scriptures first speak always and everywhere about God before they speak about us. The only really good reason to preach or to listen is the old biblical question, "Is there any word from the Lord?"

Most of us preachers probably think that our task is to bring our people close to God, to help narrow the gap between where they are and where the Bible is. But perhaps our homiletical task is sometimes to increase the distance between ourselves and the Bible, to make clear the ways in which we do not think like God, much less live as God would have us live.

> Preaching takes place from the pulpit (a place which by its awesome but obviously intentional height differs from a podium), and on the pulpit, as a final warning to those who ascend it, there is a big Bible. Preachers also wear a robe—I am not embarrassed even to say this—and they should do so, for it is a salutary reminder that from those who wear this special garment the people expect a special word. A formidable and even demonic instrument, the organ, is also active, and in order that the town and county alike should be aware of the preaching, bells are rung. And if none of these things help, will not the crosses in the churchyard which quietly look in through the windows tell you unambiguously what is relevant here and what is not?[1]

As I hear Barth on this, he is speaking up for the value of a healthy distance between where we are and where the Word of God would have us to be, a distance signified by the height of the pulpit, the dress of the preacher, the crosses in the churchyard. I pray that our preaching will

---

1. Barth, *Church Dogmatics* I/1:33.

unleash the Bible rather than make it "user friendly," overly accessible, too easily equated with ourselves and our designs. There must be some distance between the Bible and our heavily psychologized, overly politicized contemporary culture.

I could go on about our unbiblical "biblical" preaching, the way we use the text as mere pretext, the way the culture captures us on that potentially perilous way from text to sermon, the way we lust to be merely interesting rather than peculiarly biblical.

But, as Luther often said at the end of his pulpit diatribes, that will be enough of that for today.

The Wonderful Thickness of the Text!

Some summers ago, I attempted to read the Koran, the holy book of Muslims. Despite my earnest efforts, I didn't make it through the entire volume. For one thing, Mohammed, the prophet of the one true God, has an opinion on everything: how to weigh grain, how to cut meat, homosexuality (he was against it). It really is amazing how many issues there are in which Jesus appears to have had absolutely no interest.

Mohammed never tells stories. Ask him a question, he gives you a straight answer. "I have three things I want to say about how to run a government," he will say. Quite a contrast with Jesus. Mohammed always answers every question—Jesus, almost never. The Koran has a low tolerance for ambiguity, narrative, enigma; the Bible wallows in it.

When one reads the Koran, one knows immediately why there are "Muslim fundamentalists." Yet it is more difficult to understand why there are those who read, for instance, the Gospel of Luke, and find therein "fundamentals." Luke is "thick," the literature is polyvalent, predominately narrative, almost never propositional, open to multiple interpretations, defying reductionistic reading. The thick, impenetrable nature of these texts may be by conscious design. A hard-to-understand text catches our attention, begs for attention, engages our natural human inclination to figure things out. On the other hand, the texts may be difficult, obscure, and distant simply because they are talking about what is true whereas most of what we live is false. A living, righteous, prickly God tends to produce difficult Scripture.

For instance, many of us will struggle with John 20 this Easter. John first does the story of Easter as a footrace between the disciples in which they came, and then they "saw and believed" (20:8). Believed what? John says that "as yet they did not understand the scripture, that he must rise from the dead" (20:9). Presumably, they believed that the body had been

69

stolen. At any rate, whatever they believed was not yet quite Easter. Easter ends with everyone going back home (20:10) and that was that. At least the men go home. Mary stays behind to weep. She is confronted by the risen Christ, whom she regards as either the gardener or a body snatcher, or perhaps both (20:15).

Then, just to keep things interesting, John 20:19 begins Easter all over again with the story of Thomas and his doubts. Defying resolution or simple understanding, the risen Christ appears again in John 21 in a complex, utterly enigmatic appearance which becomes quite convoluted with details of fish, fishing nets, Peter, and feeding sheep.

We have a "problem" with this literature. Our problem is not, as we sometimes flatter ourselves into believing, that we are modern, critical, and skeptical whereas the text is naive, primitive, and credulous. That was historical criticism's reading of our interpretive dilemma.

No, I have come to believe that our problem is that we have become tone deaf to a text so thick, so opaque, so rich as John 20–21. We are ill-equipped to hear the Easter text. After all, we are modern, Western folk who have taught ourselves to be content with a flat, well-defined, and utterly accessible world. Our world has become "user friendly," for we can imagine no world worth having that is not subject to our utility. Our ways of knowing are positivistic, historicist, and inherently reductionistic.

Robert Alter says somewhere that, until the parables of Kafka or James Joyce's *Ulysses*, there is a sense in which we modern people had lost the skills necessary to read the Bible. Only after artists were again determined to write reality on a number of levels, exploring the complexities of human consciousness, the mystery of time, the polyvalence of words, were we able to ask the right questions of First Kings.

William C. Placher makes the evocative suggestion that the very messiness of the biblical texts—the way they parallel each other, conflict, repeat, fail to connect—is an embodiment of the God they try to bring to speech. "The narratives of this God who eschews brute force were not edited with the brute force necessary to impose a single, clear framework."[1] Just as this God, according to a number of the parables of Jesus, is willing to live with wasted seed, a net full of good and bad fish, and a garden where the weeds mix with the wheat, eschewing violent, coercive purification and harmonizing, so the willingness of the biblical writers and

1. Placher, *Narratives of a Vulnerable God*, 88.

canonizers to live with the messiness of the texts is a testimonial to their faith in a God who chooses to suffer, to embrace human messiness, and to love us in our inconsistency rather than to force us to make sense.

The interpretive skills that many of us learned in seminary invariably took a superior stance toward the text; modernity is inherently arrogant. We have been conditioned to feel that we moderns are privileged to stand at the summit of human development, uniquely equipped to stand in judgment upon any idea or anyone who preceded us. We cut apart the text, split it up into its smallest units, sever it from the community that produced it, lop off that which offends our modern sensibilities—my verbs are intentional. We are doing the same violence to the text that we do to any culture or people who are strange to us, who don't fit into the categories that we received from the Enlightenment, who refuse to produce the commodities we value.

Much of our violence begins with our modern lust for the one "right" interpretation, the one official reading. All interpretation, including historical criticism (especially historical criticism) serves some configuration of power, some social arrangement. I once thought it shameful that "uninformed" laypersons were busy interpreting biblical texts in all sorts of ways, without the benefit of academic training. I now honor such diversity of reading—particularly when they occur among folk who are not only seeking to understand the text but to embody and perform the text—as ecclesial resistance against the powers-that-be who serve the academy rather than the church.

What I am pleading for here is an interpretive approach to our Scripture that is true to the form of the Scripture itself. Just as the Koran, by its very form, renders certain kinds of readers, so the Bible, by its form, is more congenial to certain interpretive strategies than to others. The text itself encourages, provokes decentering, dislocation, and dislodgement. The very thickness of the text may be part of the text's strategic assault upon our received world.

I think we need to condition our people to expect interpretive difficulty on Sunday morning, to relish the multiplicity of messages, to love the thickness of the text, to come to church expecting to have their present reality subverted by the demanding text. Too many of us preachers say, after reading a troublesome text, "Give me twenty minutes and I will explain this for you." Even to read a troublesome text and then to say, in a well-modulated voice, "Now I have three things I want to say about this," begins to defuse the text, make it make sense without allowing the text time to make us make sense. To be baptized is to be willing to let the text stand in a superior interpretive position to us, not the other way around. Rather than treating the text like a cadaver to be dissected, we ought to pray with the psalmist, "Thou has searched me and known me, O Lord."

Easter is true because the text says it is true, because what the text says is true to the church's continuing engagement by the living Christ. It requires not certitude, the sure fixing of truth, but rather trust, a playful willingness to let the strangeness of the text have its way with us. The text has subsumed us into itself, rendered unto us a world that would have been unavailable to us without the world having been constructed (as most worlds are) by the text. Yet that does not mean that the world rendered thereby exists only in the imagination of the text. Every time the church gathers, breaks the bread, and drinks the wine, we proclaim to any who dare to listen, that what the text says, is. The text, we believe, has the power to evoke that which it describes.

We have the text, we believe, as a gracious gift of a God determined not to leave us to our own devices. What happened on Easter, namely, Jesus coming back to us, refusing to leave us alone, intruding among us, is what happens each Sunday in the reading and preaching of the text. Scripture, read and preached, is Easter all over again. And, thank God, we never exhaust the significance of it, despite our most thorough interpretive efforts, for the text and the world it renders is thick. There is always a surplus of meaning, even after the longest of our sermons.

Thus John ends his account (at least one of his accounts) of Easter by preaching,

> Now Jesus did many other signs in the presence of his disciples, which are not written in this book. But these are written so that you may come to believe that Jesus is the Messiah, the Son of God, and that through believing you may have life in his name. (John 20:30–31).

The Lectionary as a Source for Preaching:
Possibilities and Pitfalls

In Advent of 1992, the Revised Common Lectionary appeared.[1] The use of the lectionary as a source for biblical preaching texts has single-handedly led to a revolution in preaching. For thousands of congregations, it has meant that God's word is offered much more "lavishly." To extend the Vatican's culinary metaphor for the lectionary, this lavish fare is more a buffet than a banquet, a smorgasbord of texts that require discretion and judgment by the preacher.[2]

Eugene Lowry has noted how the lections lean heavily toward conclusions. They represent the end of the line of thought.[3] The devisers of the lectionary appear to love summaries, finales. Certain affirmations are simply asserted, stated out of their textual context. The narrative quality of Scripture, where texts move from beginning, to middle, to the end, is often lost as the lectionary presents us with only the end of the story, the conclusion of a passage.

Any good preacher learns to appreciate and to exploit the movement within a scriptural text. A foundational observation of contemporary homiletics is that sermons are events that unfold over time, journeys with a beginning, middle, and end. Merely to preach the end, the conclusion before one has laid the foundation, prepared the argument, set the context, is to rob the message of its power to move. The literary qualities of a text are not mere superficial adornments, but are integral to the way a text works. Therefore, when the lectionary excludes the stories of the lost sheep and the lost coin from its attenuated account of the prodigal son (Luke 15:1–3, 11b–32), something significant has been, well, *lost*. Verses

1. Langford, "The Revised Common Lectionary 1992."
2. The image is William Skudlarek's in "The Lectionary," 38.
3. Lowry, *Living with the Lectionary*, 17.

73

4–10 are not mere redundancies but progressions, active movements in a complex symphony of the lost and the found.

In many places, the lectionary seems to have a tin ear, without regard for the artistic, musical, dramatic quality of biblical texts. Scripture employs a wide range of literary devices to bring the gospel to speech. The lectionary seems in places to be based upon the now discredited historical-critical conviction that texts are mainly significant as repository of ideas, as mere containers for important propositions. Many of us preachers are learning to ask not only, "What does this text say?" but also the more dynamic, "What does this text do?" "How does the particular form of this text mean to move a congregation, then or now, from one point to another?"

Appreciation for the pacing, timing, movement, tone, and progression of a given text is too often absent from the lectionary's decisions about what will be included or excluded from a Sunday's lection. Preachers learn to be suspicious and curious whenever the lectionary omits verses from a unit of Scripture. Troublesome, incongruous, even threatening verses that challenge our systems of value are frequent victims of the lectionary's attempt to tidy up a passage.

This is not simply to admit that the lectionary is, as is any selection of Scripture, an interpretation of Scripture. Rather, it is to question the particular interpretive biases at work in the lectionary's selection and placement of Scripture as well as its omission of troublesome passages. Lectionary editors seem to be bothered by cases of biblical dissonance, conflict, violence, and oddness. Yet, most of us preachers realize that the sheer oddness of the text is often the only door we have into the composition of an interesting sermon. Preachers learn to look for that which is weird, dissonant, and curious within a biblical text as a key to homiletical engagement with the text. Thus, the lectionary is guilty of sometimes excising those aspects of the text that are the very key to the text's delivery in a sermon.

Granting the limits of lectionary, this preacher must still regard the lectionary as a great gift to our proclamation of the gospel, a revolution worth joining. Even though the lectionary committee's opinions of what to include and what to exclude in texts have been the subject of endless second guessing on the part of us preachers, the committee's decisions are, I am confident, better than mine. Time and again, the lectionary has forced me to preach from a richer array of Scripture than I would have if

I had been left to my own devices. Sunday upon Sunday, the lectionary has made me trust Scripture's testimony, to prejudice the witness of the saints of Israel and the church, and go ahead and try to preach that which, on my own, I would not have touched with a ten-foot pole, as we say in the South.

The main limitation that the lectionary has exposed is the unwillingness or the inability of us pastors to do tough biblical study in preparation for our preaching. If the use of lectionary study aids becomes an excuse for lack of critical confrontation with the text, then lectionary-based preaching may not be a step forward. Yet still, when I choose a biblical text for preaching, it is usually because I think I know what this text means and what it has to say to my congregation. When the lectionary presents me with a text, its relevance and meaning are often unclear to me. I encounter the strangeness of the text. Good things happen in a sermon when the preacher has been forced to deal with a text that the preacher finds to be not immediately congenial.

Thus, Stanley Hauerwas and I have said that we can think of no more ethically significant act than for a pastor to preach from the lectionary, to demonstrate to the congregation that we preachers did not select these texts; they selected us. We preach what we have been told to preach. In submitting to the lectionary, we demonstrate that the Bible is the church's book, that we are called as preachers to witness to the faith of the church, not our own sweet concoctions. The lectionary is one more way that we try not to think for ourselves, but to think with the saints. Thus, lectionary-based preaching makes a strong, countercultural statement about the church's peculiar notions of authority and revelation, peculiar notions that, now as then, continue to be, in their implications, revolutionary.

Parables in Our Preaching

I have sometimes said that when I was being taught to preach in seminary, I got the impression that my job as a preacher was to close the gaps. I stood in the pulpit and looked out upon great, wide gaps between me and my listeners, gaps between our time and the time of the Bible, gaps between us and God.

As a preacher it was my job, within about twenty minutes, to close those gaps, to build an interpretive bridge between my listeners and me and between my listeners and the Bible, and so forth. I was the pontifex, the bridge builder, or the mender of the gaps. The worst criticism I could imagine was when the listener emerged from one of my sermons muttering, "Sorry, but I just don't get it." It was my job as a preacher to close the gaps in understanding, to move the listener to exclaim, "I got it!"

But lately I've wondered if this is an unfair construal of the preaching task. What if my great task as a preacher is not to bridge the gaps but to open them up? It is in the gaps that we are given room to roam, space, and air to breathe. Sometimes it almost seems as if Jesus, as a communicator, does not want too quickly, too easily to bridge the gap between his listeners and the gospel. In fact, in his parables particularly, he seems intent on exposing his listeners to the gulf between their understandings of God and the reality of God.

In Year B of the Revised Common Lectionary, during which we live with the Gospel of Mark, we encounter the famous *messianic secret* that typifies Mark's Gospel. What is at the root of Jesus' reluctance to easily or quickly reveal who he is? Could it be that Jesus wants us to gain an awareness of the gap between us and God?

How to construe the gap that is the byproduct of faithful preaching? Biblical scholar John Dominic Crossan, in his book *The Dark Interval*, makes a helpful distinction between myth and parable. Myth, says

Crossan, attempts to mediate opposites, explain mystery, reconcile polarities, to take the randomness of life and weave it into a believable pattern. In myth, bad folks get what they deserve and the good are rewarded. Through myth, there are explanations for the apparent incongruities of life, reasons given by the gods.

Why is there evil in the world? Well there was this woman, Pandora (you know how nosey women are), wouldn't stay in her place, opened the mysterious box, and evil and heartache were unleashed on the world. That's why there's evil in the world. Any more questions?

Myth explains, settles, fixes, and closes the gaps in our consciousness. Crossan says myth's polar opposite is parable: "Parable brings not peace but the sword. . . . Parable casts fire upon the earth."[1] Literary critic Frank Kermode says, "Myths are the agents of stability, fictions the agents of change."[2] Parable is meant to change us, not reassure us. Parable is always a somewhat unnerving experience. The standard reaction to parable is, "I don't know what you mean by that story, but I'm certain I don't like it."

Crossan argues that myth has as its function the creation of the belief in a possibility of permanent reconciliation between the polarities and contradictions that bedevil us. Parable hopes to create contradiction within our complacent securities, to aggravate and prod us into thought and possible reconstruction of our worldview. "You have built a lovely home, myth assures us; but, whispers parable, you are right above an earthquake fault."[3]

Myth establishes world. Parable subverts world. Parable creates humility by reminding us of limits, by enticing us right up to the very edge of certitude, forcing us to peer over into the terrifying abyss of a world we do not know. Parable works the gaps in our knowledge of God, glorifies that space between us and all truth; myth reassures itself that we can and do know all we need to know and that truth is readily within our grasp.

Now ponder with me the fact that Jesus' primary, and certainly most distinctive, mode of communication was parable. What do we preachers make of that?

Jesus did not talk primarily in allegory, did not preach three-point sermons, did not offer little moralistic messages that reassured people in

1. Crossan, *The Dark Interval*, 38.
2. Quoted in Crossan, *The Dark Interval*, 39.
3. Crossan, *The Dark Interval*, 40.

their present knowledge. He told parables. In most any parable, there is a reversal of expectation, a dislocation of the hearer. Right there, at the point where conventional expectations are reversed, where the listener is dislodged, dislocated, there is the evangelical moment. There, before the abyss, the gap, God has room to move upon us and upon our present constructions of reality. Preachers who would be evangelical ought to delight in such moments, moments when parable has its way with us and we are cut loose.

In some sense, every sermon, whether it takes as its text a parable or not, ought to be parabolic, ought to provoke a confession of ignorance before the mystery of God, ought to at some point move the listener to mumble, "I just don't get it."

Preaching Parables with Matthew

I've said before that I can't figure out why in the modern period we gave the Bible to historians in order to make sense of Scripture. It's typical of the modern consciousness to act as if we have, in Scripture, a problem of mainly historical distance. We would have been on better ground if we had given the Bible to novelists and dramatists, for their work is closer to Scripture's own intentions for itself. Scripture is a complex, multifaceted, literary creation with a wide array of literary forms, including one of the New Testament's most distinctive modes of expression, the parable.

Jesus' disciples ask him in Matthew 13, "Why do you teach us through parables? Why do you teach people with stories that people can only partly understand?" If Jesus is who the voice says he was at his baptism, why is he not rousing the crowds to revolutionary action? Why tell them these enigmatic little stories that require so much reflection rather than telling them clearly and directly exactly what he wants them to know? It is as if, for some strange reason, Jesus speaks only in riddles. A characteristic Matthean means of interpretation is through parables.

Jesus' answer is almost as confusing as the parables themselves. Jesus takes them back to the Prophets, specifically to a passage in the book of Isaiah that spoke of the reaction the prophet knew his words would provoke. Isaiah knows that the people's ears are aligned against the truth of God. Great trees with roots deep in the national consciousness, stable ideas that everyone thought were self-evident and eternal, would have to come down before the new shoot of God's truth could begin to grow (Isa 10:33—11:3). God would cut the tree down, and prune it further and further, until there was nothing but a stump; but then God would reveal that there was new life hidden in the stump (6:9–13)—that amazing new life was "the holy seed" (6:13). Jesus quotes the passage in which the prophet promises that one day there will come a new seed, a new shoot that would be God's graciousness toward Israel. Taken in the context of the disciples' question about parables, Jesus seems to be making the analogy that the parables are seeds that are planted in our hearts, seeds that will bear fruit later, over time, as we live with these stories. But nothing is self-evident.

N. T. Wright, in his commentary on this passage in Matthew, says,

> The really troubling thing about this passage is not simply that people have had to wait so long to see the kingdom finally appear. The biggest problem is that, now that it is appearing at last, it is bringing both judgment and mercy. And part of the judgment is that people will look and look and not see what God is doing. People will listen and listen to what Jesus is saying and they simply won't be able to understand. Like tone-deaf people listening to a symphony, they will have no idea what it's all about.[1]

Jesus says that even this incomprehension and misunderstanding is caught up in the purposes of God. Those closest to him will understand, are just beginning to understand, though there is much still to come that they will find difficult to comprehend. Even in their incomprehension, the disciples are blessed with being able to see and hear things that God's people have desired for ages to see and hear.

But before there can be true seeing and hearing, the tree must be cut down to its stump. Judgment must fall on God's unfaithful people in order that God's mercy can grow. Wright says that hidden in this warning is the prediction that Jesus will himself go ahead of his people and take the brunt of that judgment on himself.

All this is in the future. The disciples don't understand because the parables, which are not readily available to our understanding, which challenge our securities and sureties, are themselves a form of judgment. We avoid the judgment of God above all things. We do not understand the parables, nor do we understand why Jesus has to go to Jerusalem to die on a cross. Thus this resistance and incomprehension that we find in our encounters with the parables are related to the deepest meaning of Jesus' whole ministry.

Parables, then, aren't simple uncomplicated sermon illustrations designed to help simple, ordinary folk comprehend deep theological truth. In fact, the truth they speak of is complex and deep. It is the truth about the mystery of what God is doing in our world. And it is the truth of

---

1. Wright, *Matthew for Everyone*, 160–63.

what God is doing in the life, death, and resurrection of Jesus. God is busy sowing Israel again, planting his people once more, through Jesus. But it doesn't look exactly how most people expected God to act. The parables are thus not annoying riddles but rather a complex, dynamic means of talking about a complex, dynamic subject—the God of Israel and the church.

Questions for us preachers: Can we be as complex and dynamic in our preaching as God is in God's mercy toward us? Are we willing to trust the gospel and to risk incomprehension in our hearers? Are we as resourceful as Matthew (and Jesus!) in our communication of the good news?

It Is Not Only That Jesus Was God's Son; It Is That God's Son Is Jesus: The Challenge of Incarnational Preaching

"Those who say that the God has begotten a son preach a monstrous falsehood, which the very heavens might crack, the heavens break asunder, and the mountains crumble to dust. It does not become the holy God to beget a son" (Koran, ch. 7:8).

Any God who would impregnate a poor, unmarried woman, then send a messenger to tell her that she is "blessed among women," will stoop to almost anything. That God would do such a thing seems odd to me. Yet who am I, in my limited, post-Enlightenment imagination, to tell God what God should and should not do in order to get to us?

I recall the student who came to me, distressed that he was losing his faith. When I inquired what faith he was losing, he replied, "I have problems with the virgin birth of Jesus."

I suggested that he stick with Mark for his Bible reading for the rest of the year and see if that helped, perhaps Paul too. "But don't I have to believe in the miraculous birth of Jesus in order to believe in Jesus?" he persisted.

"In one sense, no," I replied. "Yet in another sense, yes. We ask you to believe in the virginal conception of Jesus and, if we can get you to swallow that without choking, then there's no telling what else we can get you to believe. Come back next week and we'll try to convince you that the poor are royalty and the rich are in big trouble, that God not nations rules the world, and on and on. We start you out with something fairly small, like the virgin birth, then work you up to even more outrageous assertions."

As Barth said early on in his *Church Dogmatics*, "the incarnation is inconceivable but it is not absurd."[1] No pun intended, I am sure.

1. Barth, *Church Dogmatics* I/2:160.

Every three years we lectionary preachers enter Year B, Mark mostly, for the Feast of the Incarnation, which makes it a bit odd for us since, as we all know, Mark appears to know nothing of Bethlehem. Yet we shall find that Mark does know incarnation. What Luke names as manger, pregnancy, Mark speaks as an ominous, "Beware, keep alert" (13:33), or a wild voice in the wilderness (1:1–8), before he allows Luke to pick up incarnational themes in the fourth week of Advent through Christmas. Mark agrees with John 1:14 that "the Word became flesh and lived among us," though his announcement of that incarnating advent is preceded by, "Beware." I propose that we preachers take Mark's peculiar way of doing the incarnational good news as an interpretive clue to prepare to preach Christmas this year.

The main truth to keep before us, in regard to incarnation, is not that "God is with us," but that God came to us as Jesus. Of all the ways for God to enflesh, God came as a Jewish peasant from Nazareth who was murdered by the authorities, not because of the peculiarity of his birth, but for the revolutionary quality of his life. Jesus was violently tortured to death, not because he was a baby conceived out of wedlock but because of what he said and did once he grew up. His advent provoked a crisis in our settled intellectual and political arrangements, unmasking the relationship between our cherished notions of what can and can't be and our governmental sanctions about who is and who is not in charge. Luke portrays the political significance of Jesus' advent in such subtle but powerful ways, putting upon the herald angels' lips the very phrasing that had been previously used to praise Caesar. There is nothing subtle about the claims that Matthew makes with his report of the massacre of the Jewish babies. In Mark, Jesus represents a crisis from his first utterance, a continual confrontation with the powers-that-be and much blood. In short, in preparing to preach during Advent-Christmas, we preachers are in one of the most politically charged seasons of the church year. Things are getting heated, political, not simply because God came to us in the flesh but because God came to us in Jesus.

So we begin by admitting that there is this link between our incarnation and politics. Gods and kings tend to go together. Thus, I believe that Cicero, in his treatise *On the Nature of the Gods*, got it right, at least as far as first- or twentieth-century pagan alternatives go. In Cicero's century or ours, an intelligent person has only three alternatives. One can be a Stoic, believing that, although gods are not separate entities, everything is saturated with the divine. Let us reawaken the divine (whatever that is) within us and dance to the rhythm of the great oneness. Or one can be an Epicurean, believing that, if gods exist, they have little interest in us or in our world. The best course for the Epicurean is not to whine about it but rather to get on as best you can and enjoy this world as it is. Or one can be like Cicero himself, an academic, that is, a professional skeptic in service to the state. What harm is a pinch of incense or a sacrificed cock? These religious matters are awfully hard to settle, intellectually speaking, so just go along with the cultural conventions, participate in the public rituals and sacrifices, salute the flag, keep in step, because religion helps hold Rome together.[2]

Without incarnation, without a God who is passionately involved and committed to us and to creation, this is about the best that one can do, religiously speaking. All three alternatives leave the dominant political order unchallenged, even undergirded. Alas for poor Cicero, all of the beautiful pagan rituals and ceremonies, the auguries and all the rest couldn't keep Rome together. About the time that Cicero was urging his fellow Romans to keep up appearances, even if the gods might be a joke, a baby had been born out in Judea whose people would help dismantle pagan imperialism in just a few centuries. That baby brought with him, not simply a way of getting on in the world, but a whole new world, which made his virgin birth and his incarnation so much more troubling than that of Augustus.

All talk of incarnation must be kept very close to the Word incarnate, Jesus of Nazareth. If not, incarnation tends to dribble off into pantheism or vague generalities about the goodness of the world. Therefore we are privileged to proclaim, on most Sundays, that God is not merely with us, in the incarnation. God is with us as Jesus, the Word made flesh. God has a face, a name. God cannot be made into anything we like. God makes specific demands upon us, has specific expectations for us.

Mark's incarnational language reminds us: God is among us as Jesus. And that makes all the difference. Pray for the boldness to preach that difference today.

2. Cicero, *The Nature of the Gods*.

Preaching from Mark's Gospel

During Advent of year B, we find ourselves in the Gospel of Mark. If Matthew is a Gospel of enlightenment, of teaching and understanding, the Advent move into Mark's world is a journey into shadows, mystery, and tense inscrutability.

The tone is set in Mark's first parable from Jesus, the parable of the seeds, in the different kinds of soil. Jesus is like the sower who sows the seed in rather inhospitable soil. After telling them the parable, the disciples at least have the honesty to ask, "What was that supposed to mean?"

They don't understand Jesus here at the beginning. In truth, they don't understand much more of Jesus by the end, but that's still to come. Their Markan incomprehensibility is highlighted by the way the Gospel begins with a flat-out declaration of who Jesus is. Mark says that this gospel is the good news of "Jesus, the Messiah, the Son of God."

We know, up front, who Jesus is. Part of us relishes the disciples' incomprehensibility. We are already in on a secret they can't seem to figure out. Yet part of us identifies with them. We have been told that Jesus is "Messiah," and we think we know what that means. Mark rearranges our ideas of Messiah. Jesus does not play by the messianic rules. So in a sense we are one with the disciples in our confusion. We identify with their stupefied, "Who is this?"

Even though we are told that Jesus is "Messiah, Son of God," it takes eight chapters before any of the disciples get it. Then, when Peter declares, after Jesus' question "Who do people say that I am?" "You are the Christ, the Messiah," Peter doesn't say, "Son of God." We shall have to wait to find out what that means until after Jesus has suffered and died.

From these terse observations on the way that Mark does gospel I derive a couple of homiletical implications.

First, the gospel of Jesus Christ is not self-evident. It is not easy to comprehend. Partly this is because Jesus is God, a God we do not know. Partly this is because God is made manifest in Jesus, a Messiah who frustrates our messianic expectations. Any good news that doesn't entail a fair amount of mystery is not the good news as Mark presents it.

If you are a preacher who thinks your job is always to reveal, to uncover the truth and make the truth simple, plain, direct, and sure, then Year B may prove rough going for you. In Mark there is always some distance between us and Jesus, some otherness and mystery.

I wonder if people are ready for this. When I first became a pastor back in the early 70s, couples being married were always asking me for the privilege of writing their own vows in contemporary English, or using some updated, hip, marriage-a-go-go service. By the 90s, nobody asked for such services. They all wanted the traditional, Cranmerian service with its "thee" and "thou" and talk of marriage as "an outward and visible sign of an inward and spiritual grace."

Were couples now more conservative, more traditionalist, better understanding of the older Service of Holy Matrimony? I think they were now more tolerant of mystery, yearning for a thicker, richer description of their lives than they had before. They had the good sense to realize that marriage was a risky, frightening sort of move and they valued the distance, the otherness, of the older service.

If people are in the mood to take off their shoes on holy ground, to relish some of the awe and mystery of Jesus as Messiah, Son of God, then Mark makes for some great preaching.

Second, Mark's mode of gospel tends to undermine people's self-confidence that they have fully comprehended or grasped the gospel of Jesus Christ. Mark frustrates our modern attempts to collapse the gospel into the fully comprehensible, something easily explained with a few quips and slogans fit for a bumper sticker.

At the end of Mark, the women at the cemetery are told by the angel, "Don't be afraid. Go, tell!"

And then Mark says they were afraid and they didn't tell anybody! We are meant to ponder the irony, the mystery of the gap between Jesus and us, between who disciples ought to be and who they are. Things are left unexplained, undefined. Odd occurrences are left hanging in Mark. There is a kind of breathless, ragged quality to his narration of the story of Jesus. Sometimes our lives with Jesus are just like that. Here is a gospel in which the distance between us and God in the flesh is heightened, the heat is turned up, things are tense from the beginning, and even more tense at the end.

Take a moment and ponder the church being produced by reading Mark, the disciples being birthed by the story that Mark tells and the way Mark tells it. Jesus is this enigmatic figure who comes out of nowhere, not born, not from a family. He shows up at the Jordan to be baptized by John and immediately (that's one of Mark's favorite words, "immediately") there is this big bird tearing open the sky and a voice, "This is my Son, listen to him." And then immediately Jesus is cast into the wilderness where there are no words, no scripture, no Satan, just "wild beasts" with him. Welcome to Mark's world of discipleship.

My friend, novelist Reynolds Price, was being asked to name some of the great works of world literature. He mentioned the work of Dante, of his beloved Milton, and Shakespeare. Then he said, "And of course, Mark."

Mark?

"Certainly. He invented a new literary form called the gospel. If the test of great literature is to compel belief," said Price, "well then, Mark is certainly one of the greatest."

It has taken me a while to learn to appreciate the consummate artistry of Mark in telling the story of Jesus. Mark's Gospel seemed to me too primitive, dark, ragged, jarring. Then I realized Mark's intention—to render a savior who is at times primordial, inexplicable, not easily defined or contained, Lord of all, the Christ who is unknown and who stays, to some marked degree, unknown.

Pray for the grace to preach that gospel as forcefully and unforgettably as Mark.

Trusting the Bible a Little More and Ourselves a Little Less

One way to conceive of our task as preachers is that we are engaged in training our congregations to trust the Bible, to take ourselves a little less seriously and the Bible a bit more so. We gather on Sunday, the Scriptures are opened to the church, we say, "Let's all believe that this ancient book—written in a time and a language quite different from our own, by a people in many ways different from us—knows more than we." Then we attend to Scripture. Bending our lives toward the text that reaches out to us through a wide array of literary devices, thus the church is forever formed, reformed into the church of Christ.

We trust the Bible in much the same way that we learn to trust another person. William Placher notes that, when you trust someone, you know them and allow them to know you. You spend time with that person, some of it with serious intent, some of it simply to be with that person. When you converse together, because you have learned to know and to trust one another, you know that person's jokes as jokes, their tall tales as tall tales, their admonitions as words addressed to you out of love. Although we may not understand everything about that person, may not be able to connect everything that is said to us by our friend, we learn to trust that person as having our best interests at heart. We trust that we will not be led astray. We take some delight that our friend, even when we may have known her for many years, is still able to shock, surprise, confuse us because such shock and surprise remind us of the delightful, mysterious, not fully comprehensible otherness of our friend.

We trust the Bible because it keeps making sense of, as well as disrupting, the world in which we live. The Bible does not just "make sense" in the sense that the Bible is congruent with our present experiences of and definitions of reality. We must read the Bible in a way that is more careful and respectful than simply going to the Bible, rummaging about, picking and choosing on the basis of what we consider to be possible and permissible within our present context. To do so is not to align our lives with the witness of the saints, but rather to, in Barth's words, "adorn ourselves with their feathers." The temptation is to discard that which makes us uncomfortable or that which does not easily fit into our present conceptual scheme of things. Therefore, an appropriate hermeneutical question is not simply, "What does this text mean?" but rather, "How is this text asking me to change?"

Part of the joy of being a biblical preacher is that we get a front-row seat on the spectacle of the creation of a new world. The Bible wants to give us new experiences, to create a new reality that would have been unavailable to us without the Bible. The Bible does not simply want to speak to the modern world. The Bible wants to change the world, to create for us a world, through words, that would have been inaccessible to us without our submission to the text called Scripture. This is not some imaginary world. This is the real world, a world more real than today's newspaper headlines or government press releases.

And so I read in the newspaper of a woman, I think she lived in Louisiana, who had raised about a dozen foster children, despite her meager income as a domestic worker. Why did she do it? She replied, "I saw a new world a-comin'."

A major challenge for the biblical preacher is that biblical speech is not easily translated into the prevalent speech of the world. As George Lindbeck put it, when we preachers teach and preach Scripture, we engage in a complex re-description of reality in which we place present, officially sanctioned, received "reality within the scriptural framework rather than translating Scripture into extra-scriptural categories. It is the text, so to speak, which absorbs the world, rather than the world the text."[1]

My colleague Richard Lischer notes that in most of our seminary preparation, we preachers are taught to step back from the text, to attempt to assume a detached, cool, objective and dispassionate disposition toward the text. Scripture is treated as a cadaver to be dissected. In the African American church, says Lischer, the pastor attempts to step in to the text, try on the text, walk around in it, assume some of the roles that are depicted in the text. The pastor, in preaching, leads the church in stepping into the text, trying on the text, assuming a world in which the text's

1. Lindbeck, *Nature of Doctrine*, 117.

description of reality is more real than that which we typically privilege as "real."

John Calvin compares the reading of Scripture to the donning of eyeglasses that enable us to see things that, without the glasses, we would not have seen. It is of the nature of Scripture to be imperialistic, to impose a world upon its readers and hearers. Erich Auerbach spoke of Scripture as "tyrannical." Said Auerbach:

> The world of the Scripture stories is not satisfied with claiming to be a historically true reality—it insists that it is the only real world, is destined for autocracy. All other scenes, issues, and ordinances have no right to appear independently of it, and it is promised that all of them, the history of all mankind, will be given their due place within its frame, will be subordinated to it. The Scripture stories do not, like Homer's, court our favor, they do not flatter us that they may please and enchant us—they seek to subject us.[2]

We keep trusting the Bible because we keep meeting God in the Bible. In the words of Scripture, we are encountered by the incarnate Word. We call the Bible "inspired" because the Bible keeps reaching out to us, keeps striking us with its strange truth, keeps truthfully depicting God. God keeps truthfully speaking to us through Scripture as in no other medium. We trust the Bible because on enough Sundays we discover that God's Word has the power to produce the readers that it requires. In the reading of Scripture, the Creator is at work, something is made out of nothing, the church takes form around the words of the Word.

To read Scripture is to risk transformation, conversion, an exchange of masters. You might think of Sunday morning as a struggle over the question, "Who tells the story of what's going on in the world?" Scripture reading can be uncomfortable, as we are made by the Bible to see things we would have as soon ignored, as we hear a word we have been trying to avoid. Reading is not only a formative activity but also a potentially disruptive means of exiting our culture, of de-familiarizing and making the normal seem strange and the strange seem normal, of having a de-lightful respite from conventional, culturally sanctioned accounts of "the way things are." Therefore, the primary interpretive question is not, "Do I understand this passage?" but rather, "How is this text attempting to

2. Auerbach, *Mimesis*, 12.

convert me to Christ?" Behind all Scripture is not simply the question, "Will you agree?" but rather the more political, "Will you join up?"

When the authority of the Bible is challenged with "Is the Bible true?" we are not to trot out our little arguments but rather our little lives. The truthfulness of Scripture is in the lives it is able to produce.

The test for my advice on preaching is therefore not so much the eloquent sermons that it helps you to produce but rather the dedicated Christian lives that are produced through your faithful preaching. Blessings upon you as you preach.

SECTION 4

Preaching, the Church, and the World

It's About God

Paul's favorite term for the church is "the body of Christ." That is a high calling. Paul claims nothing less than that the church, your church, my church, is the physical form that Jesus takes in this world. When I think of my church (and yours!) that may seem to be too exalted a designation for us. When one encounters the grubby sociological reality of the church, as opposed to the exalted theological designation of the church, well, it can be quite disillusioning. Life in the body is tough. John says that "the Word became flesh" in Jesus Christ. Keeping the transcendent Word and the immanent flesh together in the church, that's hard. In my experience we pastors tend to get caught up so much in the mundane, fleshly, institutional, and organizational duties associated with caring for the "body"—raising money, going to meetings, keeping the roof from leaking, refereeing in congregational squabbles—that it is all too easy to lose sight that this body is nothing less than the body of Christ.

Years ago when mainline Protestant denominations began to lose members, sociologist of religion Dean Kelley published his important book, *Why Conservative Churches Are Growing*. Kelley's book was the first of an avalanche of studies on mainline Protestant church decline and Evangelical church resurgence. Among other things, Kelley claimed that the younger Evangelical churches were growing because they stressed strict doctrine, strong, even authoritarian pastoral leadership, high commitment, and other factors that were thought to be part of conservative faith.

Kelley was widely praised or condemned for this view, depending on the particular church allegiance of the critic. But these factors were not at the heart of Kelley's argument. Kelley's main thesis was that growing Evangelical churches grow because they stick to business. What is the main business of the church? Kelley put it something like this—the main business of the church is to keep referring people toward God, to keep viewing the world under God, to keep putting the God question on the table, to keep asking, in all of its thought and life together, "What does this have to do with God?" Kelley claimed that those churches grow who never lose sight of this basic business of the church. Churches decline when they forget, "It's about God."

A succession of studies has expanded upon Kelley's thesis. In their book on mainline liberal Protestantism, *Rerouting the Protestant Mainstream: Sources of Growth & Opportunities for Change*, C. Kirk Hadaway and David A. Roozen say that when all factors related to church growth and decline are studied, "The key issue for churches seems to be a compelling religious character . . . not whether the content of that character is liberal or conservative."[1]

Mainline liberal Protestantism becomes the last stop for many people on their way out of the church. Or as one of my friends put it, "Many of our people woke up one Sunday morning and just couldn't think of a compelling reason to go to church. The church had become so much like the world, why bother?"

In a more recent book by Hadaway, *Behold I Do a New Thing: Transforming Communities of Faith*, he says,

> What unchurched people are looking for is the same thing that everyone expects the church to be; a religious organization. It should look different, it should feel different, and it should sound different, because unlike every other organization in society its specialty is religion (rather than something else—group fun, golf, scuba diving, bowling, good books, etcetera). After interviewing hundreds of people in the United States and Canada who don't go to church, I have concluded that the predominant view of the church is this: It is not a particularly enjoyable group with a restricted view of morality and spirituality. Unchurched North Americans don't feel they need the church for social involvement; they don't think the church has a monopoly on truth; and they don't think the church would help them very much in their relationship with God.[2]

It is so easy for pastors to become sidetracked in our leadership of the church. In our internal maintenance of the "body," we lose sight of what the body is meant to be, how this body is different from other bodies.

1. Hadaway and Roozen, *Rerouting the Protestant Mainstream*, 69.
2. Hadaway, *Behold I Do a New Thing*, 39.

When I was a young theology professor roaming about on the weekends among churches of my denomination doing workshops on various topics of church life, I was surprised, in my conversations with laity in many congregations, to hear a frequent refrain: "We wish our pastor could be more of a spiritual leader." "Spiritual leader," what is that? In probing the laity on this matter, I heard them complain that their pastor had become little more than a manager of a volunteer organization. One layperson told me, "You can talk with our pastor about everything but God." Another said, "We asked our pastor to lead us in a Bible study and he said that he didn't have time with all the other demands of running a big church. What are pastors for?"

I expect these pastors would have been genuinely surprised to hear such a complaint from their laity. Yet the complaint is evidence that we have not been taking care of the unique business of the church.

As I consider many of the sermons that I hear and many of the sermons that I preach, I hear a decidedly a-theistic tendency. Many sermons are essentially "self-help." In too many churches that pride themselves on reaching out to "seekers" and the "unchurched," I hear sermons that are little different from the advice one could receive from any self-help book. I fear that these preachers have allowed the seekers and their limitations to determine the content of the message. We Americans are a "do it yourself" society, a people who generally believe that, if our lives are going to be better, then it is mainly left up to us to improve them. We no longer want salvation, or conversion; we want self-improvement. Jesus becomes another helpful technique, among many techniques, for getting what I want out of life before I met Jesus. Jesus becomes another "lifestyle choice" that helps me feel a bit better about myself.

The other day, watching *Dr. Phil* on the television, I at first marveled why anyone would want to put themselves through the rather excruciating critique of their lives that is offered by Dr. Phil. I heard Dr. Phil, the TV therapeutic guru, tell people things like, "You must be getting something out of your sickness, or you wouldn't stay sick." Or, "You say that you want to change your life, but you don't. This suggests to me that you are lying and really don't want to change."

Why would anybody willingly expose themselves on television to this kind of ridicule? And then I realized that Dr. Phil is really flattering us and appealing to our cherished images of ourselves. When there is no longer a God who hears and acts, then it is up to us to set our lives right or our lives won't be right. Don't pray when it is all left up to you. We have got to take matters in hand, honestly diagnose our situation, pull up our bootstraps, and move forward—on our own.

Although some sermons say that they are based on "biblical principles" or "spiritual rules for better living," in reality they are self-help, self-salvation. Christians don't believe in self-help. We believe that we cannot help ourselves, exclusively by ourselves. We need a God who saves, who reaches in, and intrudes and acts to do for us that which we cannot do for ourselves.

Too many pastors have taken our models from essentially secular images of effectiveness. We are the skillful church administrator—electronic notebook in hand, moving efficiently from meeting to meeting, getting the job done, setting goals, reaching those goals, evaluating, improving, with purpose and direction. Or, we are the therapeutic leader—helping sick people get better, offering people psychologically based techniques for self-improvement, enrolling them in therapeutic groups where the group is supposed to be their salvation. Either way, there is too little of God in these approaches to ministry.

Let's keep this about God.

Formed by the Saints

Every November we come to All Saints' Day. For some of us, in some of our ecclesial traditions, All Saints' is comparatively new to us. Saints were something that those Catholics did! Thank God, not anymore. All of us are recovering a new sense of the gift of the saints. For centuries the church has taught that the saints, those minions who surround the throne of God, help us to pray. As we pray, the saints pray with us. Our prayers are joined with that great communion who stand on another distant shore and pray with us. Now I would like to remind you that the saints, among other things, help the church to think.

This quote, which accompanied a seminary advertisement in a recent edition of *The Christian Century*, is a succinct statement of what is wrong with seminary teaching today:

> What I like about teaching theology here is the diversity of the
> student body and the openness and freedom we have as faculty in
> addressing the issues of the day in a variety of ways.

This is not original or unusual, merely typical. Left to our own devices, we seminary teachers attempt to mask the depressing sameness of our almost universally ill-formed students with talk of "diversity." We speak proudly of "openness" and "freedom" while rigidly policing ourselves for deviation from the conventional norms, as we anxiously await the world to tell us which "issues of the day" we may address in our variety of ways.

In so doing, we mirror rather than transform the seminarians whom we teach. Our difficulty is that we have students who have been formed into no specific ecclesial tradition other than the tradition that has taught them that they ought to honor no tradition. Of course, that they believe their opinions and experiences are more significant than those of the church is itself a tradition, a tradition that has characterized theological education in mainline Protestant seminaries for much of this century. So

99

the question is not, will a tradition determine how I think? Rather the question is, will the tradition that determines how I think be one that is faithful to Christ and his church?

Some theologians speak of the need to develop "critical thinking" in our seminarians, to teach them the "hermeneutics of suspicion." Criticism on what basis? Like nine out of ten average Americans, we combine radical suspicion of historic, institutionally embodied faith with a naive faith in our own ability to think for ourselves. Feminist thought has demonstrated that everyone thinks while standing somewhere, tied to some configuration of power. Or, as Bob Dylan put it, everybody serves something. Too many of us theologians have left our students to wallow in their own subjectivity rather than challenging them with a perspective not of their own devising.

I recall, some time ago, hearing Yale theologian Letty Russell speak of "theologizing from women's experience." I thought, "I hope that women have had more interesting experiences than I have had, even growing up in South Carolina." My colleague Mary McClintock Fulkerson has shown how the image "women's experience" may be merely another phase of the subjectivizing, universalizing tendencies of now discredited Western liberalism.[1] Unfortunately, what the church needs from its leaders today requires more than merely experientially based theology.

Harvard Divinity School's Jon Levenson complained that, "In an institution once explicitly and formally Christian . . . largely dedicated to the education of ministers, one can deny with utter impunity that Jesus was born of a virgin or raised from the dead. But if one says that he was the Son of God the Father, one runs afoul of the institution's deepest commitments."[2] Levenson said that the creeds of the church were now, in the hands of contemporary theological educators, no more than "a matter of personal preference."

For some years a major task of theological education, even if we have been slow to shoulder it, has been to introduce poorly catechized students to the church's tradition, to drag them out of their subjectivities toward something they could not have thought on their own.

So my colleague, Geoffrey Wainwright, rightly complains that we give him only *one* semester to teach a course in theology, covering all the ma-

---

1. Fulkerson, *Changing the Subject.*

2. Levenson, "Theological Liberalism Aborting Itself," 139.

jor doctrines of the faith, and this for those who will be ordained to spend a lifetime witnessing to the faith of the church. When Wainwright taught in the Protestant Faculty of Theology at Yaounde in the Cameroons, there his African students, for whom even the medium of instruction (French) was not their mother tongue, spent their first year learning Hebrew and Greek. For their next three years, they were required to take at least one theology course that presupposed the original languages. I suspect that the Africans have a greater sense of the church as up against something than we who, if one looks at the preponderance of therapeutically rather than theologically based courses in our seminary curricula, appear to be preparing our students for a pastoral career of helping people adjust to the dilemmas of their affluence.

As a theological educator in these waning years of the twentieth century, I need to recover a sense of myself as accountable to the church, rather than subservient to the academy. I need to listen to the church more carefully than to the alleged "issues of the day." Only then might we, as leaders of the church, be given the grace to allow our people to rise above the merely contemporary and to engage in "critical thinking" worthy of the name. Theological education begins by being formed by the saints.

You have heard me say before that using the lectionary as a resource for our preaching is a nice way of demonstrating to the congregation that we preach *what we have been told to preach.* Our preaching is not our little, personal crusade, the latest thing to emerge from the denomination's head office. Our preaching is informed, formed by the saints. Each Sunday, in submitting ourselves to Scripture, in listening to God's word in Scripture more than we listen to ourselves, we are demonstrating that we Christians think, not for ourselves, but with the saints. Through the saints, we rise above the merely contemporary, we get some big ideas, our imaginations are expanded, and Sunday becomes an adventure we would not have had if we had been left to our own devices. We pray, we *preach*, with the saints.

In my last year at Yale Divinity School, in a church history course, the professor invited an Orthodox priest who gave a rather dry lecture on the development of the creeds. At the end of the lecture, some earnest fellow student asked, "Father Theodore, what can one do when one finds it impossible to affirm certain tenets of the creed?"

The priest looked confused. "Well, you just say it. It's not that hard to learn. Most can quickly learn it by heart."

"No, you don't understand," continued the student, "what am I to do when I have difficulty affirming parts of the creed—like the virgin birth?"

The priest continued to look confused. "You just say it. Particularly when you have difficulty believing it, you just keep saying it. It will come to you eventually."

Exasperatedly, the student, a product of the same Protestant church that produced me, a representative of the sixties, pleaded, "How can I with integrity affirm a creed in which I do not believe?"

"It's not *your* creed, young man!" said an exasperated priest. "It's *our* creed. Keep saying it, for heaven's sake! Eventually, it may come to you. For some, it takes longer than for others. How old are you? Twenty-three? Don't be so hard on yourself. There are lots of things that one doesn't know at twenty-three. Eventually, it may come to you. Even if it doesn't, don't worry. It's not *your* creed."

At that moment, I realized what was wrong with much of the education I had received. A light shone brightly. I got saved from the sixties. I thanked God that, in my ministry, I was not being left to my own devices. I did not have to think for myself. Saints led the way. I could breathe.

Preaching to Young Adults

How to characterize the present age? An Episcopal priest reminded me of a scene from the movie *Jaws*, which I take to be a metaphor for us. A marine biologist arrives from Woods Hole. In a desperate attempt to find out what is going awry with the sharks in the area, a large shark is caught and brought in to the laboratory. The marine biologist lays the shark up on a table and proceeds to do an autopsy. He slits open the shark's belly. Out comes first one fish and then another. Dozens of fish are extracted. Then there's a blender and an old Florida license plate. The shark really is an eating machine.

The viewers note that the shark is an utterly indiscriminate eating machine. The shark is consuming everything in sight. Let this be a parable of modern people.

The best and the worst of a society is often mirrored by its youth. In 1994, a commission convened by the Center on Addiction and Substance Abuse at Columbia University issued a rather alarmist report, "Rethinking Rites of Passage: Substance Abuse on America's Campuses." It noted that now 1 in 3 college students drinks primarily to get drunk. Women who reported drinking to get drunk more than tripled between 1977 and 1993, a rate now equal to that of men. According to the U.S. Surgeon General, our country's college students drink nearly 4 billion cans of beer and enough wine and liquor to bring their annual consumption of alcoholic beverages up to 34 gallons a person. The report noted that college students spend $5.5 billion a year on alcohol, more than on all other beverages and their books combined. The average student spends $446 per student on alcohol per year, far exceeding the per capita expenditure for the college library.

For youth off campus, the picture is equally disturbing. The rate of violent crimes by youth in the United States rose by 25 percent during the 1980s. The teenage suicide rate has tripled over the past three decades. Suicide is the second leading cause of death of 15- to 19-year-olds.

103

A Gallup Poll found that 15 percent of American teenagers have seriously considered suicide and that 6 percent have actually tried it. Over 70 percent of teenage suicides involve the frequent use of alcohol or drugs. The image of our nation's best and brightest mindlessly consuming large amounts of alcohol is not an attractive one, yet it is an image that accurately portrays an important aspect of today's young adults. The omnivorous shark is us.

I have sometimes called today's 20-something crowd "The Abandoned Generation." Today's young adults have the dubious distinction of being our nation's most aborted generation. After scores of interviews with them, Susan Litwin called them "The Postponed Generation," those children of the children of the 60s who were raised by parents so uncertain of their own values that they dared not attempt to pass on values to their young. Recently, *The Wall Street Journal*, in an article on the shrunken futures of today's recent college graduates, called them "The Damned Generation." Not too flattering a collection of labels for today's novice adults.

I believe that communication of the gospel to this generation of young adults requires a rethinking of the task of our preaching. In speaking to "The Abandoned Generation," we are not calling them back to something they have previously known but have now forgotten; we are not attempting to open them up from a close-minded provincialism of their childhood years; we are not doing cautious Christian nurture for youth who, having been raised in a basically Christian culture, now need a little spiritual nudge to cultivate the best that is within them. We are taking people to places they have never been, calling them to become part of a countercultural adventure called discipleship, assaulting them with a weird way of configuring the world called the gospel, adopting them, giving them a new home called church.

The good news is that many of these young people are willing to listen, amazingly willing to sit still and to focus if we are bold enough to speak. What more could a preacher ask? My student generation of the 60s was unable to hear words spoken by anyone over 30. Our parents had lied to us. They did not tell us the truth about Vietnam; they failed to be straight with us about civil rights. We had to discover these truths for ourselves. If our parents had been wrong on such important issues, was there any reason to listen to them on any other major matter? Thus we saw ourselves as inaugurating the "Age of Aquarius." Everything was so fresh and new that we had to make up the rules as we went, without instruction from those who had gone before because those who had gone before had taken so many wrong turns.

But the children of the children of the 60s are more characterized by their mindless consumerism, their binge drinking on campus, and their political cynicism and disengagement than by their thoughtful struggle with the future. In my opinion, in many of today's young adults, we are seeing the results of our parenting, or lack of it. Our major educational project was breaking free of our parents, and their traditions, and their communities. Like parents have always done, we naturally assumed that our children would have the same project. We were surprised to discover what nearly every generation of parents before us has discovered—our children did not want the same world that we wanted; they did not come from the same place from which we came. We wanted to break free; our children had little need to break free (having been raised by us). Our children yearned more for roots than for freedom.

Divorce was invented by my generation sometime in the early 70s. Up until that time, this country's divorce rate was characterized by amazing stability and lack of growth. Divorce was often depicted in the 70s as the natural outgrowth of a generation come of age. Unwilling to be trapped in drab, bourgeois marriages, we would put that behind us, venture forth, be liberated, free, on our own. As a campus minister in the 90s, working with undergraduates, I quickly learned that this generation of students has a distinctly different impression of divorce. Divorce is something that happened to them when they were 12. Divorce looks different from the bottom looking up.

Because today's "Abandoned Generation" brings a new curiosity and openness to the gospel, leaders of the church therefore might need to revise some of their conventional wisdom about the imperviousness of young adult hearts to the gospel. Today's preachers must take the religious wanderings of Generation X with new seriousness. The time is ripe for new strategies of evangelization for and Christian proclamation to a generation who, having been left to their own devices, religiously speaking, now needs to be addressed by the church.

Can we see the needs and problems of this generation of young adults as an invitation to proclaim the gospel with boldness, to beckon them toward a new world named the kingdom of God? If we can, we shall discover this generation as a marvelous opportunity for gospel proclamation.

On Not Reaching Our Culture

Recently I led a group of pastors in a discussion about our preaching. When I asked the pastors, "What areas would you like help with in your preaching?" most of them responded with, "I want help in making connection with my listeners, relating the gospel to their everyday lives." "I want to preach sermons which really hit my people where they live." "I want to preach in a way that is real, that addresses the real life concerns people really have."

In sum, these pastors wanted to preach in a way that addressed their culture. There was a time when I would have agreed that this was one of the primary purposes of Christian preaching, to relate the gospel to contemporary culture. However, I have come to question this way of construing the task of Christian preaching.

Most of the preaching that I have heard in my own church family really struggles to relate the gospel to the modern world. I have come to believe that that is our weakness rather than our strength. In leaning over to speak to the modern world, I fear that we may have fallen in! When, in our sermons, we sought to use our sermons to build a bridge from the old world of the Bible to the new modern world, the traffic was only moving in one direction on that interpretive bridge. It was always the modern world rummaging about in Scripture, saying things like, "This relates to me" or "I'm sorry, this is really impractical" or "I really can't make sense out of that." It was always the modern world telling the Bible what's what.

I have come to see that this way of preaching fails to do justice to the rather imperialistic claims of Scripture. I don't believe that the Bible wants to "speak to the modern world." Rather, I think the Bible is after bigger game. The Bible doesn't want to speak to the modern world. The Bible wants to change, convert the modern world.

We, who may have lived through the most violent century in the history of the world based on body counts alone, ought not to give too much credence to the modern world. The modern world is not only the realm of the telephone, the telegraph, and allegedly "critical thinking"; this world is also the habitat of Auschwitz, two of the bloodiest wars of history, and assorted totalitarian schemes which have consumed the lives of millions. Why would our preaching want to be comprehensible to that world?

The modern world must be made to understand that it is nothing more than that—just a "world." By that I mean the modern world is an ideological construct. The modern world is an idea, an intellectual fabrication, a way of construing reality that has lasted for about two hundred years, mainly in northern Europe and some of its colonies, which now may be ending. Modernity, which held sway over human imaginations in the industrialized West for about two centuries, is now losing its grip.

Unfortunately, too often Christians have treated the modern world as if it is a fact, a reality to which we were obligated to adjust and adapt, rather than a point of view with which we might argue. Modernity has arrogance built right into itself. That is, modernity, which began as a search for certain and irrefutable knowledge, a quest for the "facts," likes to think of itself not as a point of view or way of construing the world, but simply as the facts. Therefore, all other ways of construing the world must converse with modernity on modernity's terms. Any other way of construing the world is labeled, by modernity, as being "primitive," "narrow," "tribal," or "provincial."

Fortunately, modern ways of knowing and thinking are gradually losing their privileged status in Western thought. We are realizing that modernity is only one way of describing what is going on in the world. Modernity has been a good ride in many ways. Humanity has received many gifts from modern, scientific, technological ways of thinking. However, as we end the twentieth century, we are realizing that modernity was not without its losses.

Moreover, when we speak of reaching out to our culture through the gospel, we must be reminded that the gospel is also a culture. This is only one of the problems with the attempt to "translate" the gospel into the language of the culture. As we often say, "Something is lost in translation." We are learning that you have not said "salvation" when you say "self-esteem." To have "a positive self-image" is not at all what Christians mean when we say "redemption." To invoke "the American way" is not equivalent to "the kingdom of God."

One reason this sort of translation is doomed to failure, one reason why it inevitably ends up with our preaching something much less than the gospel of Jesus Christ, is that Christianity is a culture. Just as you cannot learn to speak French by reading a French novel in an English translation—you must sit for the grammar, the syntax, and the vocabulary and learn it—so you cannot know Christianity by having it translated into some other medium like Marxism, feminism, or the language of self-esteem. Christianity is a distinct culture, with its own vocabulary, grammar, and unique practices, just like any other culture. Too often, when we reach out to speak to our culture, we merely adopt the culture of modernity at the moment, rather than presenting the gospel to the culture.

Rather than reaching out to speak to our culture, I think our time as preachers is better spent inculturating modern, late-twentieth-century Americans into a culture that is called church. When I walk into a class on introductory physics, I expect not to understand immediately most of the vocabulary, terminology, and concepts. Why should it be any different for modern Americans walking into a church?

This is why the concept of "user-friendly churches" leads to churches getting used. There is no way that I can crank the gospel down to the level where any American can walk in off the street and know what it is all about within fifteen minutes. My Lord, one can't even do that with baseball! You have to learn the vocabulary, the rules, and the culture in order to understand it. Being in church is something at least as different as baseball.

Therefore, rather than worrying a great deal about "reaching our culture," I think that we mostly ought to worry about speaking to the church, forming the church through our speech, laying on contemporary Christians the stories, images, and practices that make us disciples.

The other day someone emerged from Duke Chapel and had the audacity to tell me, "I have never heard anything like that before. Where on earth did you get that?"

Fortunately, I had the presence of mind to respond, "Where on earth would you have heard this before? After all, this is a pagan, unformed, uninformed university environment. Where would you hear this? In the philosophy department? Watching *Mister Rogers Neighborhood* on TV?

Give me a break. No, to hear this, you've got to get dressed and come down here on a Sunday morning."

It is an anachronistic, strange assumption for a contemporary American to feel that he or she already has the equipment necessary to comprehend the gospel, without any modification of lifestyle, any struggle, in short, without being born again. When you join Rotary, they give you a handshake, a lapel pin, and a membership card. When you join the church, we strip you down, throw you in the water, and half drown you. This is our way of saying, "Welcome to discipleship. Be prepared for the shock of moral regeneration and intellectual reorientation. Here is a way of life that is more than simply a different way of construing the human condition. Here is something that is nothing less than a counterculture to the one in which you have been."

The point is not to speak to the culture. The point is to change it. God's appointed means of producing change is called church. God's typical way of producing church is called preaching.

Anti-Jewish Preaching

After Auschwitz, Christian preachers are compelled to consider the ways in which our preaching, in sometimes subtle but nevertheless tragic ways, fosters contempt for God's people, the Jews. The roots of anti-Jewish preaching lie within the New Testament itself, or rather in our misinterpretations of the New Testament. Even the designations "New Testament" and "Old Testament" imply that one has superseded or negated the other, as if God has now superseded Israel and nullified the covenant with Israel by a new covenant with the church.

In many places within the Christian Scriptures, we are overhearing a painful, fierce family debate within Israel about the significance of Jesus. In some instances, we are overhearing a minority movement within Israel (the church) arguing with the religious majority (the synagogue) over who is truly faithful to Torah. It is an interpretive perversion for contemporary Christians, in our majority position, with two thousand years of Christian persecution of the Jews in our past, to align ourselves with New Testament critics of "the Jews" as if the New Testament were taking a superior attitude to Jesus' own people. It is tragic for contemporary Christian preachers to interpret the numerous prophetic rebukes of Israel, all examples of the marvelous self-critical ability of Israel, as if these rebukes were addressed to "the Jews" and not to us.

Some Jews looked at Jesus and saw the Messiah; others did not. Jesus was rejected by a variety of critics, some of whom were Jews. For contemporary Christian preachers to blame all Jews throughout history for the actions of a few of Israel's leaders at the time of Jesus is a sad misreading of history. The Jews did not kill Jesus; crucifixion was a vicious form of Roman punishment. Jesus was one of the many Jews whom the Romans martyred for their faith. For later generations of Christian preachers to somehow implicate all Jews throughout history in the death of Jesus, for the church to turn on and to persecute Jesus' own people, is a terrible act of Christian apostasy and sin against the people who taught the world to look for the Messiah and gave us God's word to show us the way.

Few Christian preachers would intentionally preach in a way that would hurt the Jews. However, there are many ways in which we are guilty of presenting Judaism in a false light:

1. Preachers will sometimes caricature the Hebrew Scriptures, saying that "The Old Testament was full of judgment and wrath; the New Testament is full of love and grace." The God depicted in the Old Testament is the same God rendered by the Christian Scriptures. The Hebrew Scriptures were the only scriptures Jesus or Paul knew. There is good news in the Hebrew Scriptures, as well as judgment in the Christian Gospels.

2. Judaism is sometimes falsely depicted as cold, dead, and legalistic. Jesus' criticism of some Pharisees in his day is interpreted as blanket condemnation of all Jews in every age. The gospel is said to have entered a religious and moral vacuum, or inflamed an otherwise dead religion. These are unfair depictions of Judaism in Jesus' day or ours.

3. The myth that the Jews killed Jesus is perpetuated when contemporary Christian preachers uncritically apply biblical passages about "the Jews" to present situations. Rather than say "the Jews" plotted against Jesus, it is more accurate to say, "Some of the authorities plotted against Jesus." Rather than say, "A group of Jews rioted against Paul's preaching," it is better to say, "Paul faced opposition from some of his fellow Jews at this synagogue."

Even though recent biblical scholarship has uncovered the true "Jewishness" of the rabbi named Jesus, the Jew of Tarsus named Paul, and indeed the close dependency of the Christian Scriptures to the faith of Israel, Christians do have major theological differences with the Jews. Those differences do not lie in our superior moral or spiritual relation to the Jews, but rather in our differences concerning Jesus. Yet after Auschwitz, after the bitter fruit of centuries of Christian anti-Jewish rhetoric, Christian complicity in the persecution of Jews, and the comparative Christian silence during the Holocaust, faithful, biblical Christian preachers must examine the depictions and renderings of Jews and Israel in our preaching, must ask the God of Israel and Jesus to purify us of our anti-Jewish past, and enable us so to proclaim the gospel in our day that our brothers and sisters in Israel see in us a better reflection of the faith of Jesus, the Jew from Nazareth.

As I consider the texts the lectionary will soon tell me to preach, I find a number of occasions that might lend themselves to homiletical interpretation that would be hurtful to the church's relationship to the Jews. For instance, I'll soon be preaching about Jesus at the wedding at Cana. The jars of water that are mentioned there in John 2 were surely jars containing the water for the Jewish rites of purification. Jesus transforms this water into wine. One interpretation might be that Jesus supersedes the old Jewish rites for purification with his new wine of the gospel. Time and again in the Gospel of John, Jesus' conflict with "the Jews" can lead today's preacher into unfair characterizations of the faith of Israel. Contemporary Christians have no temptation to elevate the ancient Jewish rites of purification over faith in Christ; therefore, for the contemporary preacher to engage in anti-Jewish polemic with this text would be very unfortunate.

Likewise, I'll soon be preaching on Luke 4, Jesus' visit to his hometown synagogue in Nazareth. For the contemporary preacher to stand beside Jesus in the pulpit at Nazareth, lashing out against these conservative Jews (I've heard this text preached in just this way) would be interpretive perversion. We are not to find our place with Jesus in the pulpit, attacking the synagogue attendees in Nazareth. Rather, we are to find ourselves in the congregation that day, with those good synagogue-going folk who are challenged by Jesus. His challenge that day was not solely against Israel, but rather against any group (like today's church) who attempts to make the living God into our tame, housebroken pet.

Jesus told the story of the waiting father (the prodigal son), which I shall also tell soon. Reading our relationship with Jews into this story, we Gentile Johnny-come-latelies into faith in the God of Israel, might see ourselves as the younger brother, the younger brother who came in from the "far country" and was invited into the party. As Gentiles, we had no claim upon the promises of the God of Israel. Yet, through an amazing act of God's grace, we were invited into those promises. The Father's party, which by rights was for the older brothers and sisters in Israel, became a party also for us.

In an act of singular theological perversion, this story took a strange turn in our day. The younger brother (we Gentiles) attempted to lock the older brother out of the party, claiming that God's grace was meant only for him (us). We Gentile Christians acted as if our older brothers and sisters were no longer in God's family. Yet the story reminds us: when we shut out the older brother, we also alienate ourselves from the Father. The story of the prodigal son ends with the younger brother in the Father's house, enjoying the party. Yet out in the darkness, standing beside the older brother, was the Father. In excluding our older brother, we had excluded the Father as well.

Can We Talk?

At universities across the country, religious diversity is one of the major changes that they are dealing with. As a former university chaplain, almost every day I came in contact with someone of another faith. But my firsthand experience of religious diversity at the university is not that unusual. Driving through rural North Carolina several years ago, I came to a little country crossroads. At the stop sign, I looked to the left and saw a sign for "The Islamic Awareness Center of Anson County." Here, in one of the most thoroughly Baptist-Methodist places in the world, was a center of Islamic faith. It reminded me of the time not long ago when I was in Iowa and discovered a community of Buddhists transplanted from Indonesia. Because you are also—wherever you live in America—part of a community that is becoming more diverse, because religious strife has become a great concern for us as a country, I thought you might be interested in a few of the things that I have learned about conversation across the boundaries of our difference. Can we talk?

Let me first say that there is a widespread misperception that religious differences are the worst sort of possible differences, the most deadly. There is a belief abroad that it is fine for folk to have differences of opinion, race, sexual orientation, and all the rest, but that somehow when it comes to differences in religion, this is particularly troublesome.

For the record let's just say that most of the bloodshed, violence, and horror that have characterized the last century has been due in no way to our religious differences. National arrogance and aspiration, economic inequities, racism, and the rise of the modern nation have been far bloodier than anything any religion has done or said. Hitler, Mao, Stalin, all killed for reasons other than religious.

I fear that there is often such concern, particularly among "sophisticated," "intellectual" folk, about religious conflict and religious differences not only because many of them know very little about religion, but also because deep down many of these folk have been indoctrinated into the belief that, after all, religion doesn't really matter, that religious devotion is some sort of primitive throwback to some earlier time and therefore is out of place in the modern world. Why would anybody kill or die for religion since we all know that religion is pointless anyway?

This is asked by the very folk who see little wrong in killing for an abstraction like "democracy," or "national security." I'm not defending violence for any reason, and I do practice a religion that specifically forbids killing, but I'm just making the point that dialog across our differences matters because religion matters, but not as the worst sort of conflict or difference that is abroad in our world.

1. Differences in religion are real and they are difficult. It's helpful to begin our conversations across our boundaries with the simple admission that our differences are real, not only apparent, that our differences are not just disagreements about beliefs but really make us very different people who think, act, and see the world in very different ways. It's no help to say, "Well, you are Jewish, I'm Christian, but when you overlook the unimportant things and look at the important things we are both very much alike." The Jew may take offense because, so often, what we consider to be "unimportant," or strange, or silly, about somebody else's faith is the very thing that holds that person's faith together. The true differences are an invitation to true conversation—respectful, attentive listening and speaking. To be in conversation with someone of another faith, to take the time to say, "Tell me about your devotion," is a recognition that his or her faith really is different from your faith and that you are willing to take the time to listen and learn.

2. People of faith have more in common with one another than with those who profess no faith. After admitting our real differences, expect to be delightfully surprised that, even though you are a Muslim and I am a Christian, there is a sense in which, in both recognizing that we are accountable to some higher power, in both believing that we are not the center of the universe, not God Almighty, that we have much in common. (I've got a Jewish friend who says that Judaism is very simple in its beliefs: (1) There is a God. (2) You are not that God.) I've seen on campus Jews and Muslims, Christians and Hindus converse with one another, complaining about their treatment at the hands of disbelieving, secular college administrators or fellow students. There is a sense in which just

being religious puts one at odds with the dominant values of the modern university campus or capitalist culture in a way that makes people of faith peculiarly united.

3. In conversation with someone of another faith, I often learn a great deal about my faith. In my own dialog with people of faiths other than my own, I don't know that I've learned a great deal about Islam or Hinduism but I sure have learned a great deal about Methodism! There is that tendency, particularly among American Christians, to think that our beliefs are fairly normal, common sense, universal, and rational. Then, in conversation with someone of another faith, we find out that we are peculiar! For instance, the notion that we should forgive our enemies, a notion that Christians talk about all the time (even if we only talk), is not found in other faiths. It's a peculiarly Christian belief. On the other hand, the Muslim is puzzled by the way that we Christians talk about the importance of prayer, but so seldom actually pray during the course of a day. Dialog is not a threat to our faith, but rather a way of deepening our faith.

I write this as we Christians are moving into a time of the year— Advent, Christmas—when we are again reminded that "the Word became flesh and dwelt among us." We believe, though not all the world does, that "Word" was not just for us, but also for all people. We believe that our good news, our gospel, is meant to be shared, enjoyed by those beyond the bounds of our faith community. So this is a great time of the year to ponder the good news as good news for all people, uniting us with our sisters and brothers, even those who don't think of us as their sisters and brothers.

So, with respect, wonder, and curiosity, with patience, expectation, and joy, let's talk!

The Particularity of Preaching

"Offer some general comments to us on the state of preaching," the letter of invitation said. "General comments." Who wants to hear general comments on anything? A distinguished theologian reminds us that there is a seductive lure in the general, the universal, and the abstract. Something within us would dearly love to keep the gospel general.

That the faith must be contextualized means that it must be made specific in relation to what is "there." Jesus commands his disciples to "love your neighbor." The Torah, which Paul claims (Rom 13:9; Gal. 5:14) is summed up in this one commandment, is as explicit as the one next door! Was it only dullness of mind that prevented Jesus' original disciples from understanding that this commandment was a universal application? Or was it something more complex than mere lack of imagination? Was it not perhaps the fact that the universal always eludes us until we can glimpse its meaning, its radicality, through the particular?

The love of neighbor as a "general" law has as frequently been used to avoid the (disturbingly specific) neighbor as to love and serve him or her. The point of Jesus' familiar parable of the Good Samaritan is lost if it is turned into a mere exemplification of the commandment to love the neighbor. If it is to achieve its intended end, the parable must function for us as a radical particularization of the commandment: "Love is not a principle which we apply, but an event in which we are involved, person with person, creature with creature."[1]

I think that's right where we preachers come in. In us, God is at work helping the gospel to become concrete, specific, particular. In our preaching, God is making an assault upon humanity's desire to keep the gospel safely confined to the general and the abstract, the universal and the ethereal.

1. Hall, *Thinking the Faith*, 149.

Recently one of you, my readers, sent me a sermon you had preached. I read the sermon. It was a good enough sermon, but still, just a sermon. Then I noticed, written at the bottom of the sermon was your note, "I preached this sermon to my little congregation in Oklahoma the week after the tragic bombing in Oklahoma City. Many in the congregation said that it was the most helpful thing they had heard all week." Suddenly this sermon was no longer just a gathering of words on a page. It was a sermon. Pictured before me was a congregation gathered, eager, confused, hungry for some word of hope and comfort. I read the sermon again and it was a totally different experience for me. This brought home to me an important truth—a sermon isn't a sermon until it takes root in a particular congregation.

As Fred Craddock once said, "Preaching is not walking through the snow without making any footprints." That is, a preacher must know that a sermon touched down somewhere, must be squarely planted upon real earth. Vague generalities are not only the death of interesting preaching, they also are inimical to the way the gospel deals with truth. Biblical truth is never about vague platitudes and high-sounding generalities. It is always incarnational—truth that touches down among a specific people, at a particular time, and a definite place. During Year C of the lectionary we read texts like:

"During the reign of Caesar Augustus when Quirinius was Governor of Syria . . ."

"It was the spring of the year, when young kings make battle . . . "

"In the year that King Uzziah died, I saw the Lord sitting upon a throne, high and lifted up, and his train filled the temple."

"And it came to pass, that while Apollos was at Corinth, Paul passed through the upper coast and came to Ephesus, finding certain disciples there."

See? Everything is quite geographically specific. There is concrete detail, mention of specific names and places. Literary theory knows that thereby narratives are given verisimilitude. Such details help to put the listener there, help the story to come alive and appear realistic. More than that, these mundane, specific, earthy details remind us that ours is an incarnational faith. Our God came to us "in the flesh," not merely hovering a few feet above the cares of this world. Our God came among us, born to a poor young woman named Mary, living in a town named Nazareth.

Luke, one of the Bible's greatest storytellers, knows that no story is worth hearing that is not specific and particular. Jesus is not the highest and best of humanity. He is a Jew. Jesus is not everywhere; he was born in Bethlehem. Again, our faith is incarnational, which means that we meet God right here, now.

Wasn't it the poet, Robert Frost, who said that we can only touch the universal by being particular? That is, a story's particularities are that which make it most applicable to the broadest range of hearers. So it can be with a sermon. Thus we don't speak abstractly of "the plight of the poor," but rather we tell what it's like to come home, after a long day of cleaning floors, and have to fix dinner for the three children under your care. We do not preach about "aging in America," but rather we tell what it's like to look on the little table by the bed and see there two forlorn Christmas cards, the last mail received, and it is now early July. Our preaching power is in the particulars.

Only you can know how your people best respond to the gospel. You live with them, day in and day out, and out of your pastoral experiences comes the unique sensitivity to their particular needs and capacities. There are many sermons that fail to hit their mark because they have not been aimed. They sound like an address on a religious subject, without any particular hearers in mind. People ought to know that, in the words of their pastor in the sermon, they have been addressed.

I am a frequent visitor in congregations other than my own. These visits have convinced me of how utterly unique and how very sacred is the relationship of the particular pastor to a particular congregation. Rarely can the material in preaching publications be used as it appears, without modification. It must be placed in context in your congregation. As editor and writer of one such resource, I cannot do that work for you. I can only hope to be a helpful colleague in that process. What a privilege it is to share in this ministry with you.

Biblical Preaching

I tend to stress the centrality of biblical preaching. Work toward a Sunday sermon begins with consideration of the biblical text. That a group of early twenty-first-century folk would gather, for about an hour, and submit ourselves to this ancient, disordered conglomeration of texts, produced by a people so different from ourselves, at a time and place quite different from our own—this is strange.

Modernity has conditioned us to think that we are privileged to live at the very summit of human development from which we look down with condescension upon everyone who arrived here before us. The Christian reading of Scripture is thus countercultural, provocative, and strange. A major task of pastors is to assist congregations in reading carefully in order to align ourselves to a text, in order to submit and bend ourselves to the complex re-description of reality that is Scripture.

In our role as interpreters of Scripture, we are heirs to Ezra. Sometime during the mid-fifth century BCE, Israel returned from exile. Their beloved Jerusalem lay in ruins. A decision was made to rebuild the walls, a first step toward reclaiming Israel's identity as a people. During the reconstruction, a scroll was found, "the book of the law of Moses, which the Lord had given to Israel" (Neh 8:1). Before the Water Gate, from morning until midday, in the presence of all the people, the priest Ezra read and "all the people were attentive to the book of the law" (8:3). Ezra stood upon a wooden platform and read. Ezra's fellow priests "gave the sense" of the words being read, "so that the people understood the reading" (8:8).

Here is a portrait of Israel at its best. The word is read and interpreted in worship, the people weep and then celebrate and align their lives accordingly. Israel is constituted, corrected, resurrected, and redeemed by words. Christian clergy stand in that place once occupied by Ezra as public readers and interpreters of Scripture. Like Israel, the church is gathered, not as the world gathers, on the basis of race, gender, nation, or class. These words of Scripture are not spoken merely in order to elicit agreement or noble feelings among the hearers, but rather to form, re-form the hearers.

It is the nature of Scripture to be *political*, that is, formative. It is the nature of Scripture to want power over our lives. So David H. Kelsey says that we come to the Bible not merely with the question, "What does the Bible say?" but also, "What is God using the Bible to do to us?" In reading the Bible, God is not merely being revealed to us, but is allowed to have God's way with us.

It is our peculiar service to the church, as its lead biblical interpreters, to lay the story of Israel and the church, as recorded in Scripture, alongside our present modes of church. Ezra did that at the Water Gate. Jesus did it in his hometown synagogue in Luke 4. In exilic conditions, the Word gathers a people. This is Israel in diaspora: the people listen, aligning themselves to the word, singing the songs of Zion, naming the name, telling the story, and thus survive as God's people.

> By the rivers of Babylon—there we sat down
> And there we wept
> When we remembered Zion . . .
> For there our captors asked us for songs,
> And our tormentors asked for mirth, saying,
> "Sing us one of the songs of Zion!"
> How could we sing the Lord's song
> In a foreign land?
> If I forget you, O Jerusalem,
> Let my right hand whither!
> (Ps 137:1–5)

Exile is not too strong a term with which to characterize the current social location of the North American church. Stanley Hauerwas and I suggested this in the *Resident Aliens: Life in the Christian Colony*, where we said that to the church has been given the task of being "an alternative *polis*, a countercultural social structure called the church . . . something that the world is not and can never be."[1]

---

1. Hauerwas and Willimon, *Resident Aliens*, 46.

The theme of exile has been extensively developed in the work of Walter Brueggemann, who reminds us that most of Israel's scripture was written by a community either in exile or coming out of exile, scripture like that found in Nehemiah. Only exilic literature could adequately express the pain and the loss felt by disestablished, relinquished Israel in the catastrophe of exile. Yet some of Israel's most assertive, visionary, hopeful, pushy poetry and prose was also written in exile, a testimony to Israel's great faith in the reign of a resourceful God who is determined to have a people. To understand how a defeated, displaced people could still express evangelical *chutzpah* in the face of Babylonian imperialism, one would have to know a God who tends toward the oppressed.

Think of all of our biblical interpretation and study as our attempt to "sing the Lord's song in a strange land."

The church is gathered by the Word. In just a few centuries the church defeated Rome on the basis of nothing more than this rather disordered collection of writings called Scripture. By water and the Word, God constitutes a family, the church. And pastors have the function of helping the church in exile read, reflect, and embody the Word of God. Our God is loquacious, creating the world with nothing more than words. Every time God's word is uttered, new worlds come into being that would be otherwise unavailable without the gift of the Word: "By faith we understand that the world was created by the word of God, so that what is seen was made out of things which do not appear" (Heb 11:3).

Scripture reading and interpretation is a challenging pastoral activity. Of course, any Christian may and should read and interpret Scripture. Yet when the pastor reads, he or she does so as priest, as the one who listens to the text for the whole church, who interprets Scripture in light of the reading of the whole church down through the ages. The pastor's reading reminds the church that the Bible is produced by the community of faith and must be interpreted within that community under the inspiration of the Holy Spirit. Since the Reformation the Bible has been abused through individual readings, readings attempted outside of the context of the church, which corrects and contextualizes our reading of Scripture. Reading in community implies the time-honored practice of interpreting Scripture with Scripture, reading in context of the whole canon, allowing individual texts to be in dialog with other texts. The Bible is meant to be read in community as the church's book, that text that both creates and critiques the church.

I am proud to be engaged with you in the task of church construction and church critique that occurs each Sunday when we pick up the Bible and begin to preach.

Bibliography

Allen, Ronald J. *Preaching the Topical Sermon*. Louisville: Westminster John Knox, 1992.

Auerbach, Erich. *Mimesis: The Representation of Reality in Western Literature*. Translated by Willard R. Trask. New York: Doubleday Anchor, 1957.

Barth, Karl. *Church Dogmatics*. Translated by G. W. Bromiley, edited by G. W. Bromiley and T. F. Torrance. 5 vols. in 13 parts. Edinburgh: T. & T. Clark, 1977.

———. *The Preaching of the Gospel*. Translated by B. E. Hooke. Philadelphia: Westminster, 1963.

Brooks, Phillips. *Lectures on Preaching: Delivered before the Divinity School of Yale College in January and February, 1877*. New York: E. P. Dutton, 1877.

Buttrick, David G. *Homiletic: Moves and Structures*. Philadelphia: Fortress, 1987.

Cicero, Marcus Tullius. *The Nature of the Gods*. Translated by P. G. Walsh. Oxford: Oxford University Press, 1998.

Corbett, Edward P. J. *Classical Rhetoric for the Modern Student*. 4th ed. New York: Oxford University Press, 1998.

Crossan, John Dominic. *The Dark Interval: Towards a Theology of Story*. Niles, IL: Argus Communications, 1975.

Dole, Bob. *Great Political Wit*. New York: Broadway, 1998.

Fosdick, Harry Emerson. *The Living of These Days: An Autobiography*. New York: Harper, 1956.

Fulkerson, Mary McClintock. *Changing the Subject: Women's Discourses and Feminist Theology*. Minneapolis: Fortress, 1994.

Hadaway, C. Kirk. *Behold I Do a New Thing: Transforming Communities of Faith*. Cleveland: Pilgrim, 2001.

Hadaway, C. Kirk, and David A. Roozen. *Rerouting the Protestant Mainstream: Sources of Growth & Opportunities for Change*. Nashville: Abingdon, 1995.

Hall, Douglas John. *Thinking the Faith: Christian Theology in a North American Context*. Minneapolis: Fortress, 1991.

Hauerwas, Stanley, and William H. Willimon. *Resident Aliens: Life in the Christian Colony*. Nashville: Abingdon, 1989.

Hughes, Robert. *American Visions: The Epic History of Art in America*. New York: Knopf, 1997.

John Chrysostom. *Six Books on the Priesthood*. Translated by Graham Neville. Crestwood, NY: St. Vladimir's Seminary Press, 1977.

Kelley, Dean M. *Why Conservative Churches Are Growing: A Study in Sociology of Religion*. New York: Harper, 1972.

Langford, Andy. "The Revised Common Lectionary 1992: A Revision for the Next Generation." *Quarterly Review* 13.2 (Summer 1993) 37–48.

Levenson, Jon D. "Theological Liberalism Aborting Itself." *The Christian Century* 109.5 (February 5–12, 1992) 139–49.

Lindbeck, George A. *The Nature of Doctrine: Religion and Theology in a Postliberal Age.* Philadelphia: Westminster, 1984.

Lischer, Richard. *The Preacher King: Martin Luther King, Jr. and the Word That Moved America.* New York: Oxford University Press, 1995.

Lowry, Eugene L. *Living with the Lectionary: Preaching through the Revised Common Lectionary.* Nashville: Abingdon, 1992.

———. *The Sermon: Dancing the Edge of Mystery.* Nashville: Abingdon, 1997.

Norris, Kathleen. *The Cloister Walk.* New York: Riverhead, 1996.

Placher, William C. *Narratives of a Vulnerable God: Christ, Theology, and Scripture.* Louisville: Westminster John Knox, 1994.

Postman, Neil. *Amusing Ourselves to Death: Public Discourse in the Age of Show Business.* New York: Penguin, 1985.

Skudlarek, William. "The Lectionary: Too Much of a Good Thing?" In *Preaching Better,* edited by Frank J. McNulty, 37–44. Mahwah, NJ: Paulist, 1985.

Taylor, Barbara Brown. *The Preaching Life.* Cambridge, MA: Cowley, 1993.

Wright, N. T. *Matthew for Everyone.* Vol. 1, *Chapters 1–15.* Louisville: Westminster John Knox, 2004.